# PRACTICAL SOCIAL WORK

### Series Editor: Jo Campling

## BASW

Social work is at an important stage in its development. All professions must be responsive to changing social and economic conditions if they are to meet the needs of those they serve. This series focuses on sound practice and the specific contribution which social workers can make to the well-being of our society in the 1990s.

The British Association of Social Workers has always been conscious of its role in setting guidelines for practice and in seeking to raise professional standards. The conception of the Practical Social Work series arose from a survey of BASW members to discover where they, the practitioners in social work, felt there was the most need for new literature. The response was overwhelming and enthusiastic, and the result is a carefully planned, coherent series of books. The emphasis is firmly on practice, set in a theoretical framework. The books will inform, stimulate and promote discussion, thus adding to the further development of skills and high professional standards. All the authors are practitioners and teachers of social work, representing a wide variety of experience.

# Working with Offenders

*Edited by*

## Hilary Walker and Bill Beaumont

364
.6

MACMILLAN

First published 1985 by
THE MACMILLAN PRESS LTD
Houndmills, Basingstoke, Hampshire RG21 2XS
and London
Companies and representatives
throughout the world

ISBN 0–333–36840–1 (hardcover)
ISBN 0–333–36833–9 (paperback)

A catalogue record for this book is available
from the British Library.

13  12  11  10  9  8  7  6  5
03  02  01  00  99  98  97  96  95

Printed in Hong Kong

# Contents

# Acknowledgements

Bill Beaumont and Hilary Walker would like to thank the contributors for their commitment to this co-operative project and acknowledge the support of others with whom we discussed the ideas in, and progress of, this book. We appreciate the efforts of all those who have worked hard to help prepare the manuscripts. Our thanks also go to Jo Campling who suggested that we might try again! Paul James's thanks go to Barbara for her support, encouragement and advice, and to Liz Harris for making sense of his scrawl and typing Chapter 8 into reasonable English. Kevin Kirwin's thanks go to all the secretaries and probation officers at Notting Hill for their help and encouragement, and particularly to Rascha Martell for typing his chapter. Also to Jean McEvoy and Jane Burke for their constructive comments on the first draft. Margaret Powell's thanks go to Anne Thomas for typing Chapter 2.

# List of Abbreviations

| | |
|---|---|
| BASW | British Association of Social Workers |
| CHAR | Campaign for Single Homeless People |
| CHE | Campaign for Homosexual Equality |
| CID | Criminal Investigation Department |
| CP | Community Programme |
| CPAG | Child Poverty Action Group |
| DHSS | Department of Health and Social Security |
| ECP | English Collective of Prostitutes |
| LAG | Legal Action Group |
| MP | Member of Parliament |
| MSC | Manpower Services Commission |
| NACRO | National Association for the Care and Resettlement of Offenders |
| NALGO | National and Local Government Officers Association |
| NAPO | National Association of Probation Officers |
| NARS | National Activity Recording Study |
| NCCL | National Council for Civil Liberties |
| NHS | National Health Service |
| NYB | National Youth Bureau |
| POA | Prison Officers Association |
| PROP | The National Prisoners Movement |
| PROS | Programme for the Reform of the Laws on Soliciting |
| RAP | Radical Alternatives to Prison |
| TUC | Trades Union Congress |
| YTS | Youth Training Scheme |

# 1

# Developing Probation Work

Hilary Walker and Bill Beaumont

In this book we hope to provide a practice text which develops and complements the ideas contained in *Probation Work* (Walker and Beaumont, 1981). There we concentrated on setting out a critical theory of probation work and were able to pay only limited, generalised attention to its consequences for a socialist probation practice. We believe that it is necessary and important to make specific and detailed links between theory and practice, and have taken the opportunity in this book to present a practice-oriented text. We have been able to gather together a group of practising probation officers with knowledge and experience of specific aspects of probation work, who share a basic political orientation. In this way it has been possible to examine different parts of the job in some depth.

When planning this book we were conscious of the potential drawbacks of using this compilation structure. We were anxious that the book should not just be a collection of loosely connected articles and through our method of working have tried to avoid this pitfall, hoping that as a result the book would be more cohesive. The group of writers assembled shared enough views to provide a base from which to proceed in a semi-collective way. We met together, circulated drafts, discussed and commented on each other's work as writing proceeded. It would have been useful to meet more regularly but limitations of time, distance and expense intervened. We are all practitioners and union activists; meetings and writing have had to be fitted into already over-committed spare time.

This meant that we were unable to work in a truly collective way, but tried to make best use of what opportunities were available. It will be evident from reading the chapters that we differ theoretically and practically on some issues. More time during meetings to debate some of these areas would have been welcome. However we are pleased that the group was able to contain any such differences and work collectively despite disagreements.

**From theory to practice**

The critical theory of *Probation Work* provides the agreed starting point for the contributions in this book. The authors deliberately concentrate on probation practice, and we were anxious that they should not have to devote space to re-stating this theoretical base. In the event some chapters, in our view, do significantly add to and develop that analysis, but all maintain a firm focus on practice issues. It may therefore be useful to start by recapping briefly on the main points of the theoretical framework which provides the common basis.

Probation officers every day encounter serious problems and dilemmas which are not readily explained. We find ourselves powerless and ineffectual in the face of the social and economic problems affecting our clients; there appear to be no real solutions; any impact we can make feels both minor and marginal; the same problems recur. The help we can offer individuals is limited, but even there we feel we are only patching up deeper problems and at worst engaging in special pleading for our clients which may disadvantage others. Many probation officers experience a divergence between their personal views and values and those they are expected to uphold in their work – they are expected to 'advertise' values of thrift, hard work, constructive use of leisure and obedience in a harsh social and criminal justice system where injustice is rife and discrimination endemic. They feel 'used' within the system, cooling out problems which require more basic solutions. Some of the structures of the job–conditions, restrictions and requirements – seem to hamper the development of useful working relationships with clients.

We identified a significant disparity between formal accounts of probation work and the reality of everyday practice. These departures reflected probation officers' responses to the problems outlined above and, we argued, represented resistance to some central assumptions in the official accounts of probation work. These rest on a consensus view in which it is assumed that all people have a shared and common interest; offenders can only reach fulfilment if in harmony with society. They are maladjusted individuals and the work of the probation service is to concentrate on their reformation into obedient and responsible citizens. Because this enterprise is seen as benefiting both society and the individual, since the path of happiness lies in acceptance of social expectations and duties, measures of care and control are seen as entirely compatible and both are justified. This relentless focus on the offender as a deviant serves the purpose of individualising widespread social problems – it is the individual, not the social system, that is at fault. Their rehabilitation is a desirable goal because it leads to their integration with society – the consensus is enlarged. In this way the probation service plays an important ideological role – by acting as the benevolent face of the penal system it reasserts the image of the 'caring' society, extending welfare from 'the cradle to the grave' even to the court and the prison cell. Finally the common image of the probation service as an independent, professional, social work agency gives way to an understanding that it is a marginal and incorporated adjunct to the state's coercive machinery, the criminal justice system.

Socialists cannot swallow the first assumption of the official account, a consensus view of society – we see society as riddled with inequality and injustice based on real, deep and enduring differences and conflicts of interests. *Probation Work* attempted to provide a coherent socialist analysis of the position of the probation service within that social system. We see it as an integral part of the capitalist state, a small cog in the criminal justice machinery. The probation service supports the dominant values of the system. Much of our work is directly determined by that relationship with the criminal justice system. We have a particular role as its 'welfare' arm which provides some discretion within which we can operate.

Nevertheless our basic duty is the transformation of the offender into the obedient citizen through obligation and co-operation secured by the exercise of mercy. Directly and indirectly our work reflects the dominant values of the capitalist system – we are to encourage our clients to accept the value of conformity, the importance of industriousness, the legitimacy of authority and the need to use leisure constructively. In some ways the practical achievement of these goals is less important than the ideological role of the service – we support the individualisation of social problems, promote the image of a humane and caring society and thus help to secure consent for the existing social system. This analysis provides an explanation for the problems and dilemmas repeatedly encountered by probation officers. Their wide-scale deviation in practice from formal accounts of the job may represent conscious, or unconscious, resistance to this structural function.

This analysis identifies some fundamental contradictions for probation officers which limit the scope for developing a progressive practice. These problems are not however very different in type or magnitude to those facing any socialist in our society. Indeed it is possible to identify room for man-oeuvre which provides potential for the development of a socialist probation practice. We do not see this taking the form of a new radical method of social work but rather an orientation, based on a socialist understanding, which involves 'examining both limitations and potential before deciding on balance what approach to adopt' (Walker and Beaumont, 1981, p. 174). Later in this book Paul Senior (Chapter 7) develops this into the notion of a 'socialist style'.

Not all contributors would agree with the entirety of our analysis but found sufficient common ground to accept it broadly as a starting point. We share an interest in developing a socialist probation practice. The inclusion of this book in a series determines its length and therefore its scope – we could not deal comprehensively with the whole range of probation service work. The topics we cover reflect two factors – areas of work which we consider significant and our choice of contributors. Each writer has, in his or her own way, taken our starting point and then sought to identify the dilemmas encountered in the area of practice chosen, weighed the limitations and potential involved and made some detailed suggestions for developing a socialist practice:

● Most probation officers still spend most of their time in one-to-one supervision. Kevin Kirwin (Chapter 3) provides a lively and readable account of this 'bread-and-butter' work. He provides a genuine grassroots account of probation work, examining the mistier areas of practice. He gently points to the ways in which he makes sense of the problems encountered and argues for a continued commitment to this unfashionable but worthwhile approach.

● Two chapters deal with probation work in the context of more powerful state institutions, courts and prisons. They have much in common and deal with the practice issues arising from our marginal position and the need to combat the twin dangers of incorporation and exclusion. Margaret Powell (Chapter 2) provides a highly readable account of the probation officer in court. She identifies strategies for maximising our impact in court duty and report writing. Nigel Stone (Chapter 4) deals with probation work with prisoners. He provides an original theoretical blend of abolitionist and humane containment approaches and from this develops a set of practice prescriptions with exciting potential. Although his conclusion supports a community-based service to prisons, he does not get bogged down in the prison welfare (in or out) debate and seeks to provide suggestions for immediate use.

● Two chapters deal with issues raised briefly in *Probation Work* which the authors were keen to develop. Hilary Walker (Chapter 5) deals with the neglected issue of women in the criminal justice system and the significance of feminist thinking for the probation service. A comprehensive review of the available evidence reveals discrimination and stereotyping in probation work and she points the way to a more balanced practice. Bill Beaumont (Chapter 6) picks up the suggestion that campaigning is an important feature of a socialist approach to probation work. Drawing on his recent practice experience in the union, he provides concrete examples of campaigning work and from these argues for a widespread and consistent engagement by probation officers in working for social change.

● Two chapters deal with important areas of new development in the probation service. Paul Senior (Chapter 7) develops his idea of 'socialist style' in relation to a particular social work method, groupwork. The use of groups in probation work is increasing and he examines the socialist potential within this method, providing a valuable guide for practitioners who wish to develop groupwork along useful and humanitarian lines. He also contributes ideas on the relevance of progressive developments in the field of education and on the significance in groupwork of 'the personal and the political'. Paul James (Chapter 8) writes about his experience in day centre work, an important growth area in probation. His chapter underlines the significance of unemployment as a contemporary issue dominating the social context of probation work. His experience is in a centre with voluntary attendance and he stoutly defends that approach against the encroachment of compulsion, highlighting its progressive potential. These two chapters open up a debate on the use of conditions in probation work which is of considerable importance.

● In a short final chapter, Bill Beaumont and Hilary Walker draw together some of the common themes arising from these contributions, comment on the 'conditions' controversy and consider the ways in which this book has refined and developed the broad practice guidelines provided by *Probation Work*.

This selection of issues inevitably leaves some glaring gaps for which we can offer no justification beyond the limits of space and the particular experience of the contributors. As in our earlier book we have omitted comment on domestic or juvenile work. We have not been able to deal with important areas of the probation service's work – community service and hostel work are the most glaring examples. We have been unable to give proper attention to race issues and their significance for the probation service and its practice. This is slowly being recognised as an important issue for probation officers and we regret this omission.

**The politics of the 'new right'**

At the time of writing (April 1984) it is clear that over the last few years considerable changes have taken place in the social, economic and political climate. Since these provide the backdrop to probation officers' daily practice, it is important to outline the main features and effects of the political doctrines of the 'new right'. These have built upon the measures and cuts already introduced by the last Labour government in the face of mounting economic pressures. Under the 'new right' these changes have significantly intensified and fundamental challenges have now been posed to the welfare state.

Economic issues, namely the recession of both the world and British economies provide the background. The Tory monetarist solution is to attempt to restructure the economy and to shift the balance of power between capital and labour decisively in favour of capital. This has meant cuts in public expenditure, high levels of unemployment, a free-market economy and a 'concerted attempt to reduce, modify and depress expectations' (Jones, 1983, p. 3). The political and social implications of this doctrine have been fundamental. The implementation of radical right policies has been orchestrated around no-nonsense, authoritarian, populist themes – individualism, minimum state intervention, the need for social discipline and authority, an efficient economy, the family, nationalism and 'law'n order' (Hall, 1983). Working people have experienced both material and ideological effects – the latter work to anticipate, justify and legitimate the former. The material impact has been felt in many ways and has affected most parts of the lives of working people. A concerted attack on the welfare state has been launched. Spending cuts in education, health, housing and social security have diminished already inadequate levels of provision. Fiscal penalties on local authorities have weakened their ability to provide services, especially for the vulnerable. Numbers of unemployed have risen sharply, together with the length of time people can expect to spend on the dole. Earnings related benefits have been phased out; the real value of supplementary benefits and pensions has been cut, while the number of special investigators has increased. The rich have been given tax cuts while a growing burden of taxation has fallen on the poor (Pond, 1983). Organised labour has been disciplined and subdued in a number of ways; the threat of unemployment, cuts in benefits, cosmetic employment schemes (YTS, CP) and through both changes in the law controlling unions and new interpretations of existing laws.

In the ideological sphere the 'new right' has worked hard to bring to the forefront, and update, familiar themes in order to make their policies appear to be plain 'common sense'. A key element has been Mrs Thatcher's nostalgic call for a return to Victorian values. Within this various aspects can be identified; individualism, nationalism, the blaming of 'outgroups' and the need for social discipline. Individualism forms part of the attack on the supportive, collective provision of the welfare state. It builds upon the unpopularity of some aspects of state services – bureaucracy, inefficiency, rigidity, inadequacy. Thus it is able to throw the emphasis back onto the alleged efficiency of free market provision and the privatisation of services; the individual being 'free' from state interference and 'free' to make a choice about acceptance of state provision (education, health care, housing). Nationalism carries the idea that in a crisis the British people can mobilise to protect their country and way of life – even if those people inhabit some small, barren islands thousands of miles away (the Falklands Factor). There is the sense that if we rally to protect our country and traditions, decline will be halted, that 'Britain is still Great, that despite change and decay we can still, when pushed, get it together' (Hobsbawm, 1983, p. 275). One aspect of this theme is that of racial supremacy; that we must appeal to the British in and amongst us – for it is that which will save us. This links with another theme, the blaming of 'outgroups' for what is going wrong. Amongst these groups, at various times and relating to different issues, are trade unions, criminals, social security 'scroungers' and black people. Finally, the need for social discipline and law and order is a powerful dimension of the 'new right' ideology. It articulates the need for 'more policing, tougher sentencing, better family discipline, the rising crime rate as an index of social disintegration, the threat to '"ordinary people going about their private business" from thieves, muggers, etc., the wave of lawlessness and the loss of law-abidingness' (Hall, 1983, p. 37). The 'new right' has constructed a moral panic by building on the legitimate concerns of ordinary people; 'if the work of the right in some areas has won support over into its camp, the law and order issues have scared people over' (Hall, 1983, p. 37). By posing issues as law and order concerns the 'new right' hàve been able to justify extensive and innovative uses of the law, especially in stifling protest and against trade unions. The law's appearance of universality and the alleged need for rigorous enforcement have been fully exploited. Despite clear political uses and abuses of the law, 'criminalisation of an activity [remains] an extremely powerful sanction and its effect is dramatic' (Walker and Beaumont, 1981, p. 134).

Having set the social, political and economic scene, it is also important to consider the potential for struggle and fightback that these conditions create. First, it is becoming increasingly apparent that the economic crisis cannot be managed by the policies and measures adopted by the 'new right'. There has been a marked failure to halt the economic decline or to remedy the weaknesses in the British economy which 'is now in a worse state than ever' (Cromar, 1983, p. 8). Tensions within the capitalist class have been created – many firms have gone out of business and a whole series of receiverships, liquidations and bankruptcies have occurred. In addition it is at least questionable whether working people will be prepared to continue to accept a worsening of the conditions of their lives – unemployment, cuts in services and reductions in living standards. Secondly, there are dangers for the 'new right' that it may fail to recognise that the order-maintaining and legitimising functions of the state need to be sustained (Lee, 1983). In their eagerness to guarantee the restructuring of the economy, the risk of a back-lash may be neglected. More oppressive measures, more cuts may overstep the limit of what will be tolerated, resulting in a strong reaction. Thirdly, although many victims of 'new right' policies appear to be apathetic and demoralised, a defence of the welfare state is underway and oppressive new measures are meeting with resistance. This fightback is limited, small-scale and generally located outside the sphere of parliamentary politics. But resentment and anger are growing and may lead to a fundamental challenge to 'new right' politics.

## The 'new right' and probation

We complete this introduction by reviewing briefly developments in, and pressures on, the probation service since 1980. Then we surveyed new developments in probation work and concluded that there was a fundamental continuity of aims between these innovations and traditional tasks and approaches. Three drifts were discernible – more extensive contact with clients, more emphasis on the use of controls and a strengthening in the ideological messages being delivered. A substantial pressure was the need to appear tough, realistic and credible to courts in an attempt to provide alternatives to custody. We concluded 'the general trend is towards the use of more coercive measures and greater restrictions on clients. The coercive tilt is likely to produce a harder probation service, servicing a harsher penal system' (Walker and Beaumont, 1981, p. 152). The evidence suggests this trend has continued and remains the prevailing tendency.

The general social pressures outlined above have had their effect on probation. The service has been largely protected from the cutbacks which have affected other public services – it has enjoyed slow growth, sheltered in the privileged 'law and order' budget. But our clients have suffered from increased unemployment, growing impoverishment and restricted access to important services like housing, education and health care. The opportunities to intervene on behalf of clients have dwindled and it has been hard to offer any antidote to depression and apathy. The probation service has been involved in the rapid growth of MSC schemes and, for many, temporary places on such schemes have replaced the expectation of full-time, permanent employment. The creation of long-term structural unemployment has slowed the growth of other employment-related probation projects and there has been a marked shift to the development of schemes linked to constructive use of leisure – 'outward bound' work is clearly back in fashion and probation clients find themselves involved in adventure sports, sailing tall ships and even parachuting!

The Criminal Justice Act 1982 introduced several legislative measures which directly affected the probation service. It represented the end of a decade of debate on measures affecting juvenile and young adult offenders but is unlikely to be remembered as a major contribution to penal thinking (Walker, 1984). Borstals were converted into youth custody centres and courts given the freedom to impose sentences of any length. This brought a welcome end to indeterminacy and the sham of 'custodial training' but allowed prison staff to retreat into uniform and produced a rapid increase in the numbers committed to youth custody. Short detention centre sentences became available; paradoxically sentencers appeared to have eschewed the 'short, sharp, shock' in favour of the longer youth custody sentences. An amendment included in the Act, to restrict custodial sentencing for young offenders to those unable or unwilling to respond to non-custodial penalties, convicted of serious offences or from whom the public must be protected, is clearly being flouted by the courts. The Act shortened the average length of licences following release from custody and replaced executive recall with a court procedure for licence breaches. Community service was extended to those aged sixteen. Intermediate treatment remained but courts were also given a cumbersome new power to make a 'supervised activity order' enabling them to specify a detailed intermediate treatment programme. The most oppressive innovation was the power to order a curfew as a condition of supervision. This new power, together with a general power to prohibit specified behaviour, has been vigorously opposed by probation officers (see Chapter 6) and appears to have been little used so far.

In *Probation Work* we commented on the development of day centres, particularly the Kent Control Unit, which adopted goals of containment. Similar developments continued but were briefly halted by a rare House of Lords examination of probation law (*Rogers* v. *Cullen*. 1982) which ruled that a condition in a probation order to attend a day centre, other than a day training centre, was improper. In delivering the judgement Lord Bridge reasserted that a probation order was made 'instead of sentencing'. Although the law appeared to allow courts great freedom in imposing conditions, these should not contain 'custodial or other elements' amounting to a sentence, nor confer unlimited discretion on the probation officer. The Home Office responded by rushing through an amendment to the Criminal Justice Act 1982 specifically allowing courts to order attendance at a day centre or other specified place and participation or non-participation in any specified activity. This catch-all new law is still to be tested to see if it displaces Lord Bridge's principles that conditions should not amount to a sentence or involve unfettered discretion. After this hiatus the drift towards increased use of conditions has resumed. Although many day centres have continued to operate on a voluntary basis, new projects tend to involve conditional attendance. Any new development which is not dressed up at least to appear, and perhaps to be, tough on probationers is in danger of being dismissed out of hand. There has been a growing tendency to require new probationers to attend 'induction groups', often backed by a condition in an order. Probation hostels have increasingly expected unemployed residents to attend training or social skills groups, sometimes as a condition of an order, sometimes as a rule of the hostel.

Towards the end of 1982, the Home Office embarked on a review of the future direction of the probation service. This political and managerial initiative has produced a 'Statement of National Objectives and Priorities' which seeks to minimise the social work role of the probation service. It suggests reduced priority for civil work and for social work with ex-prisoners, and refers to the need to establish and maintain standards of supervision which lead to confidence 'that the law is enforced' (Home Office, 1984, p. 3). These elements are consistent with the drift towards a 'tougher' probation service but the statement also includes a different and potentially competing strand also evident in the British Crime Survey. This signalled a new and more realistic perspective in the Home Office. Amongst its findings were that most crime is petty, the chances of being a victim were lower than might be expected and victims 'are less punitive towards lawbreakers than is usually imagined' (Home Office, 1983a).

The themes to emerge from this new Home Office thinking include the promotion of a more realistic presentation of crime in its social context; an emphasis on crime reduction and co-ordination between criminal justice agencies; a new interest in victim support, reparation and mediation. This new view finds mention in the Home Office priorities statement (1984) – the probation service is to contribute to 'initiatives concerned with the prevention of crime and the support of victims' (p. 5) and encourage community involvement in efforts to reduce offending. This strand sits uneasily with the remainder of the paper and goes against a trend in the probation service during the past four years when community-oriented projects were axed in favour of a narrow commitment to statutory work. The probation service in some areas has enthusiastically embraced the ideas of reparation and mediation (Harding, 1982) and some experiments have been established. It is too early to say how significant this development is or to try to place it in relation to the major drift which we have identified.

There is little ambiguity about the political pressure on the service from the new Home Secretary Mr Brittan, who is an adherent of the 'new right'. He has enlarged the prison building programme to deliver 10 600 new places and a total of 49 500 places by 1991. To compensate the 'new right' zealots for their failure to restore hanging, he imposed a minimum sentence of 20 years on some murderers, turning the clock back to 1866 (Home Office, 1979). He virtually removed the prospect of parole from prisoners sentenced to over five years for violent or drug offences. This attack on the parole system was accompanied by the extension of parole to shorter sentence prisoners through lowering the minimum qualifying period to six months. This will lead to a higher proportion of probation officers' time being spent on parole supervision. Mr Brittan has turned his attention to the probation service where he says 'it must be made clear that in every case those under supervision will meet real demands on their time, effort and adherence to the terms of supervision and that non-compliance will be dealt with firmly ...' (Brittan, 1984). The Home Secretary is constrained to be a relatively moderate spokesman for the 'new right'. Philip Goodhart,

MP, in his plan for week-long solitary confinement in rigorous conditions proposed 'a brief daily inspection, from an appropriately brusque probation officer, who would merely ascertain that the detainee was not suffering from any major mental or physical disability that required immediate treatment ...' (*Daily Telegraph*, 15 September 1983). The government is now actively considering plans to introduce parttime, periodic or weekend imprisonment with a Green Paper due in spring 1984. This is forcefully supported by the Magistrates' Association, impressed by their visit to the Kent Control and Close Support Units. These prototypes together with the fact that the New Zealand probation service runs day detention centres, have produced a real danger that the probation service will be asked to run a scheme of partial detention. Nor in 1984 can we rule out, if there is to be increasing emphasis on control and surveillance of offenders' behaviour, the future use of advanced technology. Already we have seen the Offenders Tag Association advocating the use of electronic tag devices monitored by computer, and practical experiments are under way in America (*Observer*, 10 April 1983).

The pressures from the coercive tilt upon the probation service are real and continuing. The most extreme suggestions do not have to be picked up for there to be an effect on probation thinking and practice. The terms and grounds of debate in the service have shifted enormously in the last decade. Resistance from many probation officers has lessened the effects on practice but there can be little doubt that a slow shift towards the use of more coercive measures and greater restrictions on both clients and probation officers is continuing.

# 2

# Court Work

Margaret Powell

The majority of probation officers would probably tell you
that their workplace is an office, but they are likely to spend a
significant part of the working week in or around courtrooms.
The work of the modern probation officer derives from that
of the 'police court missionary', even if many of today's
incumbents find that ancestry amusing or embarrassing. The
one thing that the many and various people who make up a
probation officer's caseload have in common is the experience of appearing in court. Much of a probation officer's time
with them will be spent discussing past, present and future
court appearances. One of the most boring parts of a probation officer's job is hanging around the court waiting for a case
you are involved in to be called. One of the most frustrating
parts of the job is to see a carefully argued social enquiry
report tossed aside after a cursory glance. One of the most
stressful parts of the job is to stand up to the testing, tetchy
and sometimes downright malicious questioning of lawyer,
magistrate or judge.

Thus, the working of the criminal courts is crucial to
probation work. The courts define, influence, disturb and
disrupt the working lives of probation officers, directly or
indirectly. The work that probation officers do in and for
courts is difficult and finely balanced – a minefield of ideological and practical problems. This chapter will seek to examine
the way courts, and particularly magistrates' courts, work in
this country, their purpose and the practical manifestation of
that purpose. It will concentrate on the position of the probation service within the courts, the work involved and the
strategies that are, or could be, used. It will mainly concern

itself with direct interaction, where the probation officer is actually present in court (on duty, or with a client) but will also touch on indirect interaction, through written reports.

## Courts: conformity and control

The laws of a country reflect the values and interests of those empowered to make the laws. Some laws reflect widely held beliefs and acquire a broad base of support. Others are much more clearly based on specific sectional interests. No law is ideologically neutral – all have a purpose, and a purpose that is to someone's advantage. Doubters should turn to the various historical studies analysing the introduction and development of particular legislation, such as William Chambliss (1971) on vagrancy or Douglas Hay (1975) on property laws. Thus, in a capitalist society, law-making has tended to strengthen capitalist interests.

The function of courts is to apply and enforce these laws, and to reinforce their own right to do so. More than anything else courts are about conformity – conformity to a system, conformity to a set of values, conformity to the structures set up to ensure conformity. Thus courts are concerned to ensure that people do not, for instance, wilfully damage others' property and that they are punished if they do; they also ensure that people continue to concede that such damage is wrong and that courts have the right to deal with those causing damage. Such enforcement requires a variety of techniques and structures of control. Whilst these include institutions such as prisons, they are also present within the courtroom itself. Thus, as well as the sentences open to them, courts have developed procedures that concentrate power in the hands of a few, that continually re-emphasise certain ideological positions and crack down hard on anyone resisting them. These procedures are often described using theatrical or games imagery (Emerson, 1967; Carlen, 1976). Such metaphors are evocative and useful as long as they neither underplay the power and coercion involved, nor the fundamental importance to the defendant of the issues at stake and the end result. Certainly, a trial is essentially about points being won by two sides using strange and complex rules. The ritual, the language, the spatial positioning of participants are so unlike everyday interaction as to seem absurd to many. The power within the court is usually held by the magistrates, although sometimes this may be usurped by the clerk. The person on the receiving end is the defendant, although such power may also be used to keep other participants (witnesses, lawyers, probation officers) in line. There is some scope for these other participants to manipulate the ritual for their own benefit, but they are essentially peripheral to the main thrust of the proceedings. Where such manoeuvring is likely to have an effect is in the interaction between the various groups of minor players. For the courtroom is also a work-place with regular workers and all the pressures of interpersonal relationships, inter-occupational rivalries, personal ambitions, inappropriate and unsatisfactory working conditions, and a burdensome workload. Individuals are seeking to maximise their influence, gain or retain power, avoid blame and clear their desks. Access to technical knowledge, access to specific current information, access to space, personal favours, threat of future disfavour, the opportunity to slow down or speed up procedure are all cards to be played in this side game.

Back in the main arena, the position of workers such as probation officers is marginal, and there are dangers for those on the margin of powerful institutions. They tend to draw you in, take you over, incorporate you into their own structures, or exclude you, ignore you, write you off as an irrelevance. To avoid one or other of these fates is difficult but necessary for the probation officer trying to work in a progressive way.

**Probation officers in court: a description**

When I joined the probation service more than a decade ago, 'Court Duty' impinged on my life and my diary about once a fortnight. It meant remembering to wear a skirt. It meant a day away from the office, which had to be planned for, and a pile of messages to be dealt with on my return. It meant working through my lunch-hour in an effort to keep up with the paperwork. It meant a day of rush and scurry and hasty conversations and lost papers and queues for the telephone and looking for people who had already gone, in the organised chaos that typifies a busy inner-city magistrates' court.

On paper, the job seemed fairly straightforward. Get the court list of those appearing that day and check it against office records to see who might be known. With any luck, the clerical staff will have done this before you get there. Check that any social enquiry reports due to be submitted that day are ready, or at at least said to be on their way. Make a note of any requests or comments thrown your way by colleagues ('Make sure John Smith knows he's due to see me tomorrow'; 'If they want a report on Sally Jones they really ought to ask for a medical report as well'). Get across to the court building. Find defendants on whom reports have been written and make sure they have seen them. Find their solicitors and let them have a copy. Keep a note of the results of cases. Present reports and feed information to the magistrates as appropriate ('There is a bail bed available at . . .'). Note information that needs to be passed back to colleagues. Complete request forms for reports. Offer immediate help – or at least a calm and clear explanation – to the distressed and uncomprehending ('Now, your husband will be taken to the prison and you'll be able to visit . . .'). Give instructions to clients, old and new ('Mr Brown would like to see you tomorrow afternoon'). See those sentenced, or remanded in custody ('Is there anyone who needs to know where you are?'). Make the phone-calls, write the letters, send off the report requests, fill in the diary, have a cup of tea.

Of course, it was not as easy as that. Reports were lost in the post. Papers got mislaid. In a grossly inadequate building, people were not easy to find. Quiet places in which to talk were at a premium. Telephones were never available when you needed them. Lawyers and magistrates asked the questions you could not answer. Staffing levels on the rota were difficult to get right – have someone in each court and you found yourself twiddling your thumbs during a long, contested case riddled with precedent and references to appeal court decisions; have someone covering more than one court and you were rushing from one to the other trying to do several things at once. And there were local variations. We were often asked to help find accommodation, unlike the court up the road. We seldom did 'put-backs' – the instant interview and verbal report much appreciated by the court down the road. More pertinently, there were variations between individual probation officers. Some were sticklers for accuracy in the paperwork but seldom spoke to anyone. Some missed crucial dates but spent a long time with defendants, their families and friends. Others gleaned all sorts of useful information from solicitors, gaolers and clerks. Some were anxious, hesitant, inaudible in the appalling acoustics of the courtroom. Others were gregarious and jovial, swopping gossip with all and sundry. Some kept a low profile, literally kept their heads down, in order to avoid involvement and possible confrontation. Others were interventionist, on their feet, offering their services, imposing their presence and their opinions on the proceedings.

There have been changes since then. Probation ancillaries began to be appointed in large numbers. Whilst their role was often ill-defined and their aspirations confused, there is no doubt that they became heavily involved in court duty. In the mid-1970s, the notion of the 'court team' emerged. In some areas a team of probation officers, plus senior and ancillaries, were assigned to cover a magistrates' court on a permanent basis. These were full-time court duty officers, previously a rare species only occasionally found in crown courts. In addition, they usually wrote social enquiry reports (to the extent of being 'intake teams' in some areas) but rarely carried case-loads of any significance. In some parts of the country the court duty rota has virtually disappeared, with only occasional Saturday and Bank Holiday duties lurking in the worker's diary as a reminder. These changes have a significance that will be returned to later, but I believe my earlier description holds true, especially for those busy city courts where I, like the majority of probation officers, have worked.

It is worth adding, however, that probation officers have an alternative experience of being present in court. For a generation of probation officers working in areas where there is a court team, it is the only experience. It is attendance at court with a client, and especially to present a report. The task is a different and much more specific one. The stress is associated with long hours of waiting, not hustle and bustle. The feeling of fear of being put on the spot is likely to be greater. The known defendant has a direct outlet for his or her emotional response, be it fear, anger or relief. The analysis that follows will examine the position of the probation officer in court in a way that encompasses both court duty and attendance for a specific purpose.

## Court duty: an analysis

The difficulty of court work for probation officers lies both in the role and in the tasks involved in that role. The marginality of probation officers to the main purpose of courts has already been mentioned. Concern for the defendant (and why be a probation officer unless you have some concern for the defendant?) can make the injustices and harshness hard to take. Probation officers in court have knowledge of particular defendants, and have a general understanding of the impact of a court appearance on defendants and the implications of various sentences. To give a simple example, probation officers who spend much of their time dealing with the financial problems of their clients are acutely aware of the impact of fines. The formal definition of the probation officer as a 'social caseworker who is an officer of the court' (Morison Report, 1962) does not really assist anyone struggling to balance the conflicting demands of court and defendant and to avoid the dual traps of incorporation into or exclusion from a coercive institution. Probation officers tend to resolve that dilemma in different ways. One analysis (Carlen and Powell, 1979) has categorised the following approaches – 'servant of the court', 'political educator of the magistrates', 'McKenzie friend', and 'independent professional'. The latter was the definition preferred by probation officers, whilst the third (McKenzie friend – a lay person speaking on behalf of the defendant) was the one most commonly attributed to them by others in the courtroom including the defendant.

Earlier, the court was described as a workplace. Probation

officers are one of the occupational groups within the courts – along with clerks and lawyers (defence and prosecution), policemen (gaolers and warrant officers as well as arresting officers, CID and traffic cops), ushers and even journalists. Within this group of workers probation officers are in a relatively disadvantaged position. They have little with which to barter for power and influence. By and large, probation officers have less technical knowledge than clerks and lawyers and, often, policemen, and may need to seek advice. What technical knowledge they do have is highly specialised and can only be used infrequently. I once heard a probation officer trade opinions with a Law Lord about the length of an after-care licence, but similar opportunities are rare and perhaps even more rarely taken. The probation service's technical knowledge, such as it is, only comes into its own with a change in the law, like the introduction of community service. Even then, many probation officers are strangely lackadaisical in their efforts to master this knowledge, despite the usefulness of such expertise.

Probation officers in court *do* control a certain amount of current information – especially in the form of social enquiry reports. In many courts this is exploited in dealings with defence lawyers. However, attempts to control this information are often simply bluster, based on the festering antagonism of probation officers towards lawyers who use reports rather than preparing a plea of mitigation properly. Balancing the information controlled by probation officers is the information they need to get from, or at least check with, others. This means ensuring access to the holders of that information and securing their willingness to share it.

Probation officers do not control important space. Indeed, I have known courts where they have been unable even to preserve the exclusivity of the probation bench. They need access to space controlled by others – especially behind the scenes in the clerks' offices or the cells – and that can be denied. Even if allowed, the power of others can often be easily emphasised – as in the 'accidental'' locking-up of all new probation officers in the cells of one court known to me, which had virtually become an initiation ritual. Similarly, probation officers have little or no control over time, and limited opportunity to influence the order of business or the speed of the proceedings. Probation officers also have to cope with the stylised language and ritualised behaviour of court proceedings without the training and experience of lawyers or the police. The probation officer's knowledge of defendants, and sympathy with them, may mean they are particularly vulnerable to the rigorous enforcement of style and ritual. I recall the sharp rebuke delivered to a probation officer, trying to hustle the agitated family of a defendant out of court, for failing to bow adequately to the Bench.

For all these reasons, probation officers trying to do their job in court can feel frightened and overwhelmed by manifestations of power. They can feel frustrated and angered by what goes on; anxious about their vulnerability. They may feel relieved that their relative weakness means that little is expected of them. Some may even welcome this disadvantaged position in that it identifies them with the defendant, brings them closer in their powerlessness. Whilst the danger of exclusion is real, probation officers are not necessarily as helpless as they may appear. Courts need the opportunity to show mercy and display humanity, and on these occasions will turn to the probation service. There are also times when the defendant will display such distress, anger, confusion or irrationality that the court has to turn to someone believed to have the skill and experience to cope. On these occasions, the probation service comes into its own.

Over the years, probation officers have developed strategies to strengthen their position, which individuals use to varying extents. It is possible to make the best use of the knowledge and information held. It is possible to develop an understanding of what is going on, and to use that understanding to develop confidence and minimise fear. Probation officers give considerable thought to their performance in court, and this often centres on such issues as dress. Presentation can become more authoritative by developing skills in public speaking, being clear and concise in a formal public setting. It is possible to establish productive personal relationships which minimise the disadvantages of having limited automatic access to knowledge, information or space. We can build on a reputation for doing the basic job efficiently and good-naturedly; no-one gives much credence to the slapdash or ill-tempered. It is possible to strengthen our position by way of a collective approach, by ensuring the support of colleagues, by establishing a consistent probation presence and denying the opportunity for individuals to be picked off.

If such strategies are used carefully, it is possible to develop a probation presence in court which is confident, clear as to its purpose, offers a proper, non-deferential service to magistrates and humane, purposeful support and help to defendants. Regrettably it is also possible to use these strategies simply to minimise stress on probation officers. If an understanding of what is going on enables the conscientious to be available to intervene at the right time in the right place, it also enables the less conscientious to be at the other end of the building. Good personal relationships and a cheerful demeanour can simply keep everybody happy without exploiting that goodwill to any positive purpose. Probation officers' skill at dealing with the distressed and angry can be used to 'cool out' emotion instead of channelling it to a purpose. A collective approach can be collective apathy.

Within this discussion of how court duty can be performed it is necessary to look at the position of specialist court teams and of ancillaries. Court teams were set up to improve the work done in court by establishing a group of people familiar with the proceedings, with maximum knowledge and understanding, who could develop a considered and consistent approach. This should open up the way to a high-profile, positive, innovative presence in court from the probation service. This has not always been the result. Because court teams work relatively regular hours, without case-loads and out of the mainstream of probation work, they may attract the less energetic rather than the explicitly innovative, for whom there are less structured, more prestigious settings. The daily grind can mean that team members become more concerned with the processing of work than with the quality of the outcome. Getting through the list becomes more important than what actually happens to people. Finally, probation officers working within a powerful and all-encompassing institution like a court risk over-familiarity to the point of incorporation. The dangers here are similar to those faced by probation officers working in prison. A degree of familiarity, understanding and trust is necessary to get the job done, but can easily take over so that the primary loyalty is to the institution and not to the client or even colleagues outside. Thus, many court teams appear not to have fulfilled their promise.

Whether or not specialist court teams have been established, probation service ancillaries now undertake a significant amount of the court work of the probation service. The introduction and growth of the ancillary grade has been viewed by some probation officers with suspicion. Others were only too happy to hand over jobs they regarded as tiresome or stressful. Yet others were (and still are) concerned about the level of remuneration offered for the level of responsibility expected, and the limited training opportunities and career prospects. Although ancillaries in court are as good, bad or indifferent in their job as their probation officer colleagues, and although they adopt many of the same strategies, it does seem as if their involvement has emphasised the administrative and clerical aspects of the work. Individuals may successfully resist it, but the way ancillaries have been introduced does tend to suggest that many probation managements have put the emphasis on the paperwork rather than the client, and increased the risk of incorporation into the court system.

## Court duty: positive practice

Earlier parts of this chapter have identified strategies by which probation workers in the court setting can establish a base from which to work effectively and influence proceedings. Court duty has to be taken seriously as a task that requires skill and understanding and not simply an ability to fill in forms. It is a job for which time needs to be put aside, not simply an extra tacked on to a full working week. It is necessary to develop confidence through understanding and clarity of purpose, but also by ensuring the support of probation colleagues and by acquiring the skills that enhance a public performance. Confidence can provide the thick skin that is necessary so that rebukes and snubs do not deter. We need to develop contacts and networks so that the administrative side of the job can be done well and is not easily sabotaged. Competence and goodwill are powerful tools for those attempting to infiltrate a hostile or potentially hostile environment. Conflict is less destructive if you can show that you are also useful.

From such a base, it is possible for the job as presently defined to be done well – to provide the court with accurate and helpful information about defendants and the impact of sentencing; to provide colleagues with information and a channel of communication; to deal with immediate problems (practical and emotional) arising out of a court appearance; to enhance understanding of the probation service and what it has on offer.

It is also possible to extend the definition of the job. Probation workers can strive for clarity and fairness and as much dignity as possible for the defendant. Probation officers and ancillaries should be scrupulous in their dealings with defendants who ought not to be fobbed off with partial explanations, short-changed in terms of time or help, or bombarded with questions within earshot of all and sundry. It is significant that we tend to talk of defendants having 'seen' a report – is not the purpose to *read* it? That requires peace and quiet, and assistance for those whose reading ability is limited. Moreover, if probation workers are to be sources of help and explanation they themselves need to be accessible and identifiable. Have you ever walked into a strange court and tried to find the duty officer? Have you as duty officer ever been mistaken for a lawyer, police officer or a defendant? Clear identification of the probation bench and the probation office in the court would be a starting point.

Having established a standard of behaviour by example, it is possible to move on and, with some trepidation, make demands of others. It is not easy, but complaints about the rudeness of officials are necessary. The complaint may relate to the way you are treated; a colleague of mine was sarcastically criticised when passing information to the court from another agency. Later she quietly and politely pointed out that, whilst annoyance at the content of the message might have been justifiable, rudeness to the messenger was uncalled for. The complaint may relate to the treatment of defendants; a team, for example, that becomes aware of a consistent pattern of unhelpfulness from the Fines Department, or high-handedness from the ushers, can share their perceptions with the appropriate administrator. The incomprehensible gabble that passes for explanation from some clerks needs to be pointed out. The perversity of some sentencing needs to be confronted. This may happen immediately, or by way of subsequent meetings. It requires confidence and courage, and both can be bolstered by support from colleagues and, where appropriate, from the union.

It is also possible for probation workers to improve the service to clients by declining to cover up obvious deficiencies. Probation workers should be highlighting the need for proper duty-solicitor schemes instead of offering off-the-cuff legal opinions themselves. Probation workers should be arguing the case for creches instead of looking after young children whilst their parents are in the courtroom. They should be thinking carefully about how often they 'cool out' difficult situations, instead of leaving the responsibility for decisions clearly with those who have made them.

Finally, the probation officer has a foot in the outside world as well, and can make use of it. There is the possibility of injecting some awareness of the realities of life into the workings of the courtroom. Probation officers are in a position to make it clear how much it costs to rent a room, how long it takes to get a council flat, what the chances of getting a job really are, what living on DHSS benefit actually means. They are also in a position to feed back to the outside world what actually goes on in court – and this is now happening more frequently. The publicity given to the fate of those caught up in the 'Operation Major' raid against claimants in Oxford in 1982 owed much to the local probation officers sitting in court. The treatment meted out to prostitutes both before and after the Criminal Justice Act 1982 has been put into focus by probation officers using their court-based experience. A drive by NAPO early in 1984 to publicise the increasingly harsh treatment of fine defaulters drew its information from probation officers in court in various parts of the country. NAPO in association with other organisations, has sought to use court duty officers to monitor the sentencing patterns of black defendants. More is happening, but much of the potential is as yet untapped.

## Court reports: the indirect presence

The writing of social enquiry reports brings probation officers much more on to centre stage and, indeed, their influence on proceedings reaches its greatest potential. Here, also, the dual dangers of incorporation and exclusion are best recognised. Most probation officers are acutely aware of the danger of writing something totally unacceptable to the court in terms of content or style which will be scornfully disregarded. Widely acknowledged, but perhaps more difficult to recognise in your own work, is the habit of 'second guessing' – anticipating the court's intention and going along with it. For this reason, figures showing high take-up rates on recommendations have to be viewed with some caution. However, it is possible to pick a way between these two traps and probation officers will identify with pleasure those occasions when a 'difficult' recommendation has been accepted.

Most working probation officers recognise the complex and ambiguous nature of social enquiry reports and much of the research undertaken in this field is oversimplified (Pearce and Wareham, 1977). Statistical surveys and structural responses (verification of information, sub-headings, proformas) have little meaning. Report writing is about getting a result, and getting results involves the use of strategies. These have been described in various ways (Pearce and Wareham, 1977; Carlen and Powell, 1979) but all involve the selective use of information and the careful choice of words and concepts to get a desired result. When the explicit recognition of such strategic writing is felt to be unwise or potentially embarrassing, it can easily be justified in terms of 'keeping it relevant' or 'personal style'.

The use of social enquiry reports in the sentencing process

and the techniques adopted by probation officers in writing them produce many traps for the unwary. The criminal justice system, because it seeks to uphold the overall social and economic structure, is intent on identifying and in dealing with offenders in terms of personal culpability. Social enquiry reports are an important part of this process of individualisation. Similarly, because the system needs to distinguish between individuals in order to justify the different sentences imposed, reports are powerful identifiers of 'moral character', on which to base variations. Because the courts respond to simple ideas and because the tread-mill of writing reports saps the imagination, it is easy for them to become cliché-ridden. The stereotypes of the feckless drunk, the inadequate mother and the hostile adolescent are only too easy to trot out time after time. As well as feeding into existing images, probation officers may contribute towards establishing new stereotypes, in the way they deal with particular, emergent groups (such as squatters, punks and Rastafarians).

As well as their concern with individual moral character, reports tend to reflect the wider set of values that courts seek to uphold. Thus jobs, homes and families are good things. Hedonism, rootlessness and absence of ambition are all viewed with some suspicion. Unorthodox views (be they social, political or religious) can be made to seem almost pathological. Reports can also reinforce the attitudes of the court towards types of law-breaking ('The Bench will no doubt be taking a very serious view of this offence. . .') and adopt the court's values in terms of expectations of the defendant ('Despite this, Mr Brown shows very little remorse'). All this means that, deliberately or not, reports can become a coercive tool – conform to the correct stereotype and a 'good' report will get you a lighter sentence. Reports can become part of the process of humiliation that courts use to emphasise their power. Being discussed, being evaluated, being judged, can be an uncomfortable experience at the best of times. Seeing one's life history, failings and mistakes baldly stated in type is painful. Reading the unexpected, not knowing why certain things have been said, seeing the report being flipped through with idle curiosity by the duty officer, must all rub salt into the wound.

**Court reports: positive practice**

As with court duty, probation officers may be wary of adopting strategies (or of admitting that they adopt strategies) aimed at getting recommendations accepted, because they dislike the sense of collusion and are fearful of incorporation into the system. As with court duty, the strategies, selection of information and choice of language, can be used to safeguard the probation officer's own position, to gain 'credibility' and avoid conflict. However, if used carefully and deliberately, they can maximise our effectiveness as probation officers in a way that is beneficial to defendants.

In reports, it is hard to avoid the process of individualisation altogether and clumsy resistance ('getting political') is a certain route to exclusion. It is possible, though, to put an individual's circumstances in a broader context, to link individual behaviour with economic conditions, social structures and cultural traditions. For example, with a little extra effort, a description of an individual's search for work can be directly related to precise figures on local unemployment obtained from the Department of Employment, or exact details of the availability of re-training opportunities and the waiting lists involved. Similarly, it is very difficult to avoid all reference to the dominant value system and equally difficult to avoid clichés and linguistic conventions. Thus, it is important that the defendant knows what is going to be said, understands why, and has apparently critical comments explained. Remarks that are simply derogatory cannot be justified. Whilst a certain amount of strategic stereotyping may need to go on, there are less justifiable, more intrusive images that need to be eradicated. Elsewhere, in this book, Hilary Walker examines stereotypes of women and looks at how sexist attitudes need to be challenged. Similarly Pat Whitehouse (1983) has examined social enquiry reports, for racist attitudes. He has also described how a series of workshop discussions using actual reports enabled probation officers to examine their own racism (intentional or otherwise) and to develop ways of writing reports that do not disadvantage the black defendant. These workshops need to become more widespread, but such collective examination could also become part of a team's normal practice as a whole group, or by using a 'pairing' or 'shadowing' system. Clearly there is potential here for using the same learning technique more widely on other issues. Attitudes based on stereotypes are at their most dangerous when they express themselves in sentencing recommendations – black youths who are too 'difficult' for probation or women for whom community service work is 'unsuitable'. It is important that probation officers do not jump to conclusions but retain an open-minded approach towards deciding which defendants are suitable for a particular disposal. We may need to improve facilities if certain groups (for instance, those with children needing creches) are disadvantaged.

Sentencing recommendations present other openings for positive practice. In a system geared towards incarceration it is necessary to exploit every possible opportunity for mercy. Courts are willing enough to imprison defendants without the support of probation officers who neither offer non-custodial alternatives, nor point out the limitations of custody (Lacey, 1983). It is important to avoid recommendations that push defendants up the tariff and inexorably lead towards imprisonment. Probation officers have sometimes recommended suspended prison sentences as though they provided a non-custodial sentence; such recommendations clearly fall into this category. So do recommendations for community service as an alternative to a fine rather than to custody, however attractive such recommendations are when dealing with the impoverished for whom spare time is more realistically available than money. We should avoid recommendations that are unecessarily complicated, such as those that add formal conditions to the basic probation order, instead of negotiating details of the help available, and the commitment required, with the individual defendant. We must also avoid recommendations for conditions that are based on false premises and may be unworkable, such as curfews.

## In conclusion

In this chapter aspects of the everyday, taken-for-granted work of probation officers have been examined. The difficulties that arise from working on the margins of a powerful institution have been identified. Just because it is everyday work, it does not need to be ordinary or uninspired. Just because it is difficult, it ought not to be avoided. Even in routine work and in oppressive surroundings there is scope for positive practice.

# 3

# Probation and Supervision

Kevin Kirwin

The past twenty years have seen a considerable growth in the functions and responsibilities of the probation service. We now find probation officers staffing the welfare departments of prisons and involved in conciliation schemes; there are hostels and day centres run by the probation service; probation officers have had to absorb an increasing amount of work resulting from prisoners released on statutory licences. The methods of working have also changed: probation officers can be found working in pairs or groups, and with pairs or groups of clients. The arena in which this contact takes place has changed as well, and nowadays we can sometimes be found in community centres running coffee mornings, or doing outreach work 'on the streets'. Every summer the mountains of Wales hum with the sound of probation officers and their clients involved in outdoor 'activities' in the countryside.

Other pressures for change have been increasingly felt by the probation service over the last few years, in the form of stricter controls in probation orders, additional conditions and calls for tightening up, with more people taken back to court for breaches. The sentencer now has a whole armoury of conditions, requirements and curfews that can be imposed in addition to the 'basic' probation order. If these were to be widely used, the autonomy of both officer and client would be severely curtailed. Widespread resistance by probation officers has meant that use of these new measures has been kept to a minimum, so the legislative changes have not yet had a great effect on the practice of probation officers in most parts of the country.

Despite these pressures, new locations and methods of working, the 'bread and butter' work of the probation service with which most of our time is involved remains for many of us – the one-to-one supervision of offenders in the community on probation and supervision orders without any additional conditions. This type of work has been unfashionable for nearly a decade now, and several of the changes described above have come about at least in part through pressure from within the service for ways of working which are believed to be more effective or involve greater job satisfaction. What follows is written in the belief that there is value in this 'bread and butter' work, providing a flexible sentencing alternative to the courts, which is humane and at least as effective as any other sentence.

This chapter is to a large extent a description of the way probation officers supervise their clients. It is based on my own practice and that of other officers with whom I have discussed probation work. It is hopefully an account of a fairly typical way of working, in which others will find echoes of their own experience, but I recognise that wide variations exist. I am not attempting to describe an ideal way of supervising clients, but to offer an account of what actually takes place in supervision and how I make sense of the problems we face. This is offered as an antidote to the bulk of social work literature which tends to describe not what we do, but what we might do or ought to be doing. It describes how we meet clients, talk with them, try to help them and some of the constraints under which we operate.

## Meeting clients

There are a variety of ways in which someone can end up under supervision. A court can make an 'instant' order, without a report, after a brief interview by the court probation officer. Clients can be transferred from a departing colleague, a student or another area. An order may be made following a pre-trial report to a crown court. These ways have their own particular dissatisfactions for probation officers. 'Instant' orders can lead to unwilling or inappropriate people being placed on probation, causing problems later. 'Transfers' are notoriously difficult as you try to handle invidious comparisons with the previous worker – this god-like creature who used to visit every week, was incredibly helpful and sympathetic, and had an unending supply of money there for the asking. Pre-trial reports can often involve a lengthy wait between interview and court appearance, during which enthusiasm for the experience of supervision can sometimes wane, for both parties.

By far the most common way in which someone is placed on probation or supervision is following a remand for reports at a magistrates' or juvenile court. The magistrates may think they do not know enough about this person to deal with him or her fairly; they may think that there are problems with which a probation officer may be able to help; they may be baffled as to how to sentence and want a second opinion; or they may even simply wish to overcome legal restraints on sending the person straight to prison. The probation officer and the person on remand meet during this period, and as a result a report may be prepared recommending a probation or supervision order. This may in turn be accepted by the magistrates, who make an order for a period from six months to three years. Whether the recommendation is accepted will be in part determined by the initial reasons for remand, but other factors will come into play – the strength of argument behind the recommendation, its feasibility in the eyes of the magistrates; how 'realistic' it is in view of the nature of the offence and the criminal record of the offender; and the personal predisposition of the sentencers. A probation officer may make the recommendation for a variety of reasons – because they think the person they have met needs 'help'; because, given all the circumstances, they believe that a probation order would be a 'fair' way of dealing with the case; to keep someone out of prison; or because they do not know what else to recommend. The potential probationer will also have an influence on this process – some people will ask to be put on probation, others will vehemently oppose the idea. Very few probation officers will recommend probation for someone they actively dislike. Most will be reluctant to recommend it for someone who shows little enthusiasm for the prospect.

## Honesty with clients

In spite of the rather haphazard nature of this process, it is something over which the probation officer can exercise a considerable amount of influence. A consistent theme of this chapter is the importance of being honest with clients about what being on probation involves. This is critically important during the remand period, when the decision whether or not someone is to be recommended for probation is made. Probation can be made to sound rather austere and threatening ('you will have to come to see me every week or you will be taken back to court') or delightfully beneficial and rewarding ('I will be able to help you with the housing department, DHSS, get you some money for clothes'), depending upon whether the client is being encouraged or discouraged.

The reality is usually neither as austere nor as enticing as either of these extremes, and people who may be placed on probation deserve enough information on which to base a decision. Probation officers know how they work and can prevent nasty surprises or disappointed expectations by explaining their role, without threatening or promising too much or too little. There may be an obvious temptation to discourage someone that you actively dislike and think you could not bear to see for the next two years. But someone else in your team might not have a strong aversion to them, and it is worth discussing such cases with the rest of the team. If that produces no response, then you may need to persevere in order to avoid unjust discrimination. My own impression is that more people are inappropriately encouraged than discouraged. The probation order began as a direct alternative to imprisonment and remains usable in this way. However, it is a currency always in danger of devaluation by over-use, particularly if consistently recommended for first- or second-time offenders not remotely in danger of imprisonment. Much of this inappropriate use of orders is made where someone is seen to need help, without considering whether it can be found elsewhere, or given by a probation officer without an order. It is useful to consider this in discussion with the client and to point out the consequences of possible future offending during a probation order. It is usually possible to have a recommendation for probation accepted if someone is in breach of a conditional discharge, but much more difficult to get a conditional discharge for a breach of a probation order.

Although the decision about whether to accept being placed on probation can be something of a Hobson's choice, clients should know, before they consent, what is expected of them in terms of frequency of contact, home visits, and in what circumstances they may be in danger of being breached. They should also be told that records are kept on them, and whether or not they will be allowed to see them. I would also add that we are supervised by our management, and their case may be discussed during this supervision. Many clients have little initial curiosity about records, because they do not know they exist. Once they do know, they often want to see everything, even reading through copies of letters to themselves with intense absorption. Opening records up can be a good discipline; sloppy judgemental statements will quickly be cut out if you know you may have to answer for them later.

Probation orders carry legal penalties for failure to co-operate. Clients have a right to know what they are and that these penalties could potentially be used against them. They also ought to know that if they offend during the course of an order, a separate penalty can be imposed for the breach of probation. Clients may need to be reminded of our ambiguous role within the criminal justice system – some things that they could tell you might make it difficult to preserve confidentiality. Such situations do not often arise but you should try to alert your clients to the danger, so that they are forewarned. Probation officers are often keen about clients getting their legal rights in other fields; it is only just that people under their authority know exactly what they are up against.

Whether or not to breach someone is a more thorny problem, and an issue which often comes up in discussions between probation officers, management and courts. Nevertheless, I doubt whether it is as much of a problem privately as it seems publicly, because the vast majority of us rarely breach anyone. When we do, it is often because the person on probation has disappeared without trace fairly early in the order, and we take out a warrant to protect ourselves (from the possibility that the failure to supervise will be discovered). If you know where someone is, the problem of breaching does not usually arise. Someone who is not co-operative, but continually offending, will be dealt with by the courts without the probation officer initiating proceedings (and may well start coming to see you to get a 'good' report). Other clients who are not co-operative can usually be worked with in some way and where even this fails you may be able to make a case for early discharge, or the substitution of a conditional discharge.

**Talking with clients**

Probation officers spend a significant amount of time talking with their clients. The probation order obliges clients to visit or receive visits from their probation officers. There is no legal obligation on them to talk to their officers, or the probation officers to them, but both sides usually make considerable efforts to try to find some common conversational ground. If the weather, television, sport, the court appearance or finding out what has happened recently fail to produce a response, the relationship can become so embarrassing that either side will soon start opting out – the client by failing to keep appointments, or the probation officer by not offering them. This can provide a useful topic of conversation in its own right, as in 'why haven't you been keeping your appointments?', or 'what have you been doing since I last saw you'. In order to fill up uncomfortable silences I have developed the art of the 'sit-down comic'; if people have to come to see me, at least they should be entertained. When this is flagrantly unsuccessful the interview can be brought to an abrupt but dignified conclusion by promising to write with a fresh appointment 'in a few weeks time'.

Providing some form of informal counselling, emotional support or sympathy has always been an important aspect of our work. Just how significant a part is open to some question, and I would agree with Walker and Beaumont (1981) that its relative importance has been overstated. Nevertheless there are opportunities for important and useful work. During the course of an order our clients may be concerned about the whole range of worries and difficulties that may affect any of us – family problems, trouble with partners or any other type of personal distress, and if they want to discuss these matters with us, we should give them the opportunity to do so. In this way we may be able to reduce anxiety or distress, and sometimes help to point to ways forward. Probation clients commonly have particular worries related to being processed through the legal system. One common instance is with first offenders, who during a remand for reports are often terrified that they are going to be sent to prison. A probation officer, knowing his or her own court, can often give reassurance based on experience that this will not happen.

The notion that the art of being skilfully sympathetic can be elevated to an elaborated 'science of casework' has a lengthy history in social work literature. At its most extreme it seeks to create a 'medical' model of social work. When this is transplanted to the field of probation, clients are to be 'cured' of delinquency through casework. As this model is going out of fashion even in probation management circles, I will not take up space here on a critique of it.

The probation service, like any other organisation, has its zealots, and in my five years as a probation officer, I have probably come across advocates of most of the myriad of social work theories that have been in and out of vogue over the last 30 years. However, the majority of officers, once the effects of their social work courses have worn off, seem to treat their clients in a sympathetic, caring and overwhelmingly straightforward manner, free from the devious tricks of social casework taught in the textbooks. If someone comes in upset, they will try to comfort them. If clients need someone to talk to, probation officers will listen. They actually share a joke and laugh with their clients. Together they will spend time talking about everyday matters. In essence, we talk about more or less what everyone else talks about. Yet, there is a great sense of guilt about this in the probation service, which I think needs to be dispelled. There is a powerful ethic that heavy 'casework', deep-end therapy is work and that talking to people in a normal human way is not. I have been away with mixed groups of probation officers and clients and can bear witness to the fact that they all talked to each other quite normally. Afterwards I was worried that when they got back to their offices, they were all practising skilled casework again, apart from me. The way to consistently combat this feeling is to talk honestly to other probation officers about how you, and they, deal with clients – and then to try to stop feeling guilty about it.

Being treated in a normal humane manner is often a pleasant surprise for those clients who have been previously treated to the exigencies of the 'deep' case-worker. This style of working is also a positive antidote to another pressure that bears on the officer–client relationship – the need to encourage conformity to a set of values promulgated by the criminal justice system. The courts do not simply deal with breaches of laws made by parliament, they also stand for a positive ethos of conformity. This involves accepting authority, living in a family (being married with children or living with parents), using leisure time constructively, being in full-time work or education. Because of their relationship with the courts, probation officers can consciously or unconsciously transmit these values in their work with clients. Issues about acceptance of these values can intrude into discussions with clients, but this should be resisted.

Most clients realise the importance of these values and recognise that, when appearing in court, having a job or a promise of one, going back to school, getting married, having children are all positive indicators, and may have almost as much effect on sentence as the nature of their offence. In their reports, probation officers pick up these positive indicators and often link them together with a conclusion concerning the client's chances of keeping free from further offending. However, outside the constraints of the court setting, probation officers have more autonomy in discussing these issues. If clients want help getting a job, I will do what little I can to assist. If they do not want to discuss this area of their life, I will not constantly depress them with the fact of their unemployment by bringing it up every time I see them. I think that more recently, many probation officers have also adopted this approach. A recognition of the enormous difficulties of obtaining employment, and disillusionment with the value of

MSC schemes, have led to a lessening of the pressure to find work. Instead attention has shifted to the 'constructive' use of leisure time, particularly with young people. More energy is spent setting up projects and persuading clients to take part; sometimes through the use of extra conditions in supervision orders. This use of conditions is unnecessary and unhelpful. If my clients express an interest in trying out new and different leisure activities then I would try to encourage them, help them find appropriate facilities and seek some financial assistance for them. I try to avoid nagging them about how they spend their time, and criticising their choice of pursuits.

Another pressure of the criminal justice system I try to avoid when talking with clients is individualisation, so that they don't see their situation and the problems they face as unique to them. It is important they can understand that their difficulties are shared – both with offenders and other working-class people. These discussions raise political issues which can be connected to clients' own experiences. This can be a useful process which, through increasing understanding, helps to prevent clients from feeling totally responsible for their situation. Differences are bound to arise between you and some clients, for example over sexism and racism. I think it is important to try to deal with those differences in an open and honest way although this will not be easy or straightforward. Another problematic occasion when it is important to tackle issues in an honest manner is if a client's behaviour gives serious cause for concern. We should then explain clearly why we are worried, give the client an opportunity to put his or her position, and be genuinely prepared to consider that when deciding on a course of action.

### Helping clients

One concept which consistently appears in descriptions of our job is that we are 'helpers'. Magistrates put people on probation so that we can 'help' them; we say in our reports that someone might benefit from the 'assistance' of a probation officer; some crimes are referred to as a 'cry for help'; the public believe we 'help' people who 'get into trouble'; and clients may ask 'can (or how can) you help me?' In some cases the very act of having someone on probation is sufficient help in itself, in that the person will have been saved from going to prison. In others, talking with clients may be enough. However, there is also a significant group of people who will come to the probation service requesting practical and financial assistance.

Probation officers spend a significant amount of time in negotiating on behalf of clients with other agencies – phoning and writing to the DHSS, housing departments and fuel boards or arranging nursery places. They may not have privileged access but are fairly experienced in handling them and do not find them particularly daunting, and their position as probation officers gives them a credibility which can be useful to clients in getting a better service. It is much easier to have someone to deal with a monolithic bureaucracy on your behalf than to tackle it yourself, especially when it means not having to use coin-box phones that jam up or swallow all your money. People also seek help when their own dealings with these departments have been unsuccessful and they want the additional weight of a probation officer to back up their case. Such work is not very popular among probation officers, which is perhaps why my social work course taught me to treat these requests with a degree of wariness. It was argued that they were probably only the 'presenting problems' of a much greater malaise (for example, family breakdown or psychosis), which needed to be tackled instead. Other reasons for not dealing with these requests were that you were taking away the clients' responsibility for coping with these departments; not helping them to acquire the necessary skills; and by encouraging special treatment for *your* clients you were helping them to queue jump.

If someone asks you to phone the DHSS for them, go ahead and do it. If they have taken the trouble to come to see you and perhaps waited around for you, then you owe it to them to accede to this straightforward request. Even if all they want to do is save money by using your phone, what is so wrong in that? If someone wants a special case made for their rehousing, then as far as you are honestly able to, do it. Most probation officers, moving to a new home without a 'phone, would be prepared to ask their senior to write a letter saying that they need a phone urgently for work. If *you* can queue jump to get yourself a telephone you can write a letter setting out truthfully, but forcefully, your client's housing problems without considering everyone else on the housing list. It is not enough in these areas of welfare rights and housing advice just to meet clients' simple requests for help. You owe it to your clients to know enough about these issues to help them work out if they have a good case, to make their case well, and on the most promising grounds, and to help them pursue it, or at least to know how to refer them on for specialist advice and representation.

The problem with this whole issue is that there are not enough of these services to satisfy everyone, and even where services exist they are often not of the right type or quality to meet people's needs. There is scope within the probation officer's job to campaign for more and better resources (see Chapter 6), and plenty of opportunities to discuss with clients why particular facilities are not available (local authority priorities, government cutbacks and so on). When faced with requests for help which cannot be given, or demands for services which are unavailable, it is important to be realistic and honest about the possibilities. Youngsters who are unhappy at home sometimes commit offences and are put on probation. They ask if I can get them a flat and a job. I tell them no, but that I might be able to get them into a hostel or onto an MSC scheme. In all these cases I feel as if I am short-changing them. They have expectations which perhaps ought to be met, but which I cannot fulfil. The second-rate alternatives are there, but they have probably already been considered and rejected. This is why I always try to let clients know early on what I may or may not be able to do, so that no-one is lured into accepting supervision under false premises. A generalised offer of assistance, without a description of what that help might be – and its limits – can lead to an initial enthusiasm which quickly vanishes.

The other main type of practical assistance involves the giving of money to clients. There is a fairly wide variation between probation areas and even within offices, in the way money is dispensed. However, in my experience there are some common ground rules which operate, regardless of these differences. Most probation officers will supply small amounts of cash as fare money, or bus or train tickets. This could be interpreted as a belief that travel broadens the mind, but it often has more to do with getting someone off the premises in a way that is mutually acceptable to officer and client. Drug addicts, gamblers or alcoholics will rarely get money for any purpose, although they will sometimes be given fares if thought to be travelling to a worthwhile destination (hostel, hospital or DHSS). Anyone with children, even addicts with children, will have a good chance of getting money, either from a sense of compassion or an uneasy conscience at the possible consequences of refusal. Outside of these areas, the whole issue becomes much more difficult. I have given money to someone for a deodorant, but refused to buy someone else a jacket. Would you help someone buy a wardrobe if they already had a cupboard? Is a television a necessity or a luxury? If you would not give someone money for drink, would you for cigarettes? My experience suggests that these decisions are made in the light of various factors – how important the probation officer believes the request to be, how much effort it will take to get hold of the money, their judgement of the client's character and the persistence of the client's demands.

Although we do not have great financial resources, we generally have a flexibility which would be the envy of some social workers and DHSS officials, in whose offices money can only be given out within strictly operated bureaucratic criteria. There is a belief in the service that to frequently give out money is in some way unprofessional – in fact I remember in my early days regaling colleagues with stories of how I refused people money, to win their approval. Then I found out that whatever they said publicly, they were willing to respond to requests for financial help quickly and without a great deal of suspicion and questioning. They would even give people a second chance when they had previously had money and spent it on drink. I followed their example and believe that it is absolutely right to give out money in this way. It may be true that in many cases this money should have been given by the DHSS but if this is so you can always try to claim it back from that department. If you are prepared to help people out financially you should tell them that when they are put on probation. Where I have not done so, I have occasionally found people who have endured real hardship without realising I might have been able to help.

**Practical constraints**

Some of the constraints within which we work have already
been mentioned. In some areas the debate about whether or
not to give money may mean little, as there is hardly any
money to give. All of Britain has been affected by cuts in
welfare services, housing and social security spending, so the
margin of discretion in which a probation officer can lobby for
an individual client is rapidly shrinking, as the general level of
resources decreases. In a probation or supervision order,
officer and client are committed to keep in contact for a fixed
period of time, there are penalties for non-compliance en-
forceable by the courts, and probation management exert an
influence over the quality of this contact through record-
keeping and supervision.

One of the other constraints on probation officers' work is
the time available to see people on probation. The Home
Office's National Activity Recording Study (1977) found that
the average time spent on a probation order was two and a
quarter hours per month; only half of that was actually spent
in contact with the client and others in the client network.
This suggests that anyone whose case-load is over the average
of 35 will have less than an hour's contact a month with their
probation clients. There will be, of course, variations around
this average figure between probation officers, different
clients and at various stages in orders. I know from my own
experience that there are times when you may be seeing a
particular client for a considerable amount of time every day,
when a severe crisis is occurring in their lives. On the other
hand, I have had people in the latter stages of their orders
where the months have been punctuated by only a couple of
phone calls and a five-minute interview. In looking at my own
work and from discussion with other officers, an hour a month
does not seem a wildly inaccurate norm. There are ways in
which this limited amount of time seems to be a real constraint on the work we do. In social work literature there is a
great emphasis on the importance of the 'relationship' between social worker and client. How strong a 'relationship'
can be built up and maintained with the limited amount of
contact we have with some clients? I would contend that you

are likely to have a rather marginal place in someone's life if you tend to see them for less time than they spend talking to the hairdresser or greengrocer. These time constraints certainly make the notion of social workers acting as therapists for their clients a rather unlikely proposition.

Every survey that has been done on the subject has shown that probation officers work more than their contracted hours, and there is certainly some room for lightening the probation officer's load by the provision of extra staff. I also believe that governments cannot keep piling extra responsibilities upon the probation service without the quality of our work suffering. However, if my caseload were suddenly to drop I know that I would use the extra time available visiting people in prison more frequently, spending more time on social enquiry reports and doing follow-up work after interviews more promptly and thoroughly. Some probation clients would also be seen more frequently, but not that many. There are several reasons for this. There are clients who do not come in willingly. With them I have reached an acceptable compromise between their reluctance to come in and my wish to maintain contact which results in regular but not too frequent reporting, thus keeping both of us fairly satisfied. I do not offer them many appointments, but if they manage to keep these, I am content. There are others who may have had particular problems at the beginning of the order, which are now sorted out. They are unlikely to re-offend, and they might quite willingly come in more often but there would be no real point in this as we have not got much to discuss together. Some clients suffer regular crises and will instantly and consistently seek my help in dealing or coping with whatever has happened. I usually have no choice but to find time to help them out, whatever else I might be doing. Finally, there is a relatively small group of people with whom I could valuably spend more time. They are people who may have a whole series of problems, or be in a particularly vulnerable situation, but will rarely contact me, even when things have deteriorated to an intolerable degree. I try to visit them frequently and regularly and am concerned if pressures from other areas of my work do not allow me to do so. It is particularly infuriating if you find yourself helping someone deal with the consequences of something you might have been able to prevent if you had been able to see them the week before.

Another related difficulty is the availability of probation officers. The NARS study (Home Office, 1977) also found that officers spend under 30 per cent of their time supervising clients. If you have a problem with which you need help unexpectedly you may find your probation officer involved in any of the other duties they have to perform, and consequently out of the office or unavailable. 'I kept ringing, but you never seem to be in' and 'Why are you always in meetings?' are common complaints. If you want to see a probation officer urgently and your own is not available, you will usually have to go to the office during strictly limited duty hours and argue your case with their reluctant and case-hardened colleagues who are on the lookout for a 'con-artist'. There may be times when this relative inaccessibility is annoying or even have serious consequences for the person involved, but generally this is not the case, because the probation service is not the supplier of essential services such as housing, fuel or medical care. Some money is available for particular groups of people but no-one can demand money as of right, and there is no appeal against refusal. The probation service runs some accommodation, but mostly in hostels, run on rehabilitative or semi-therapeutic lines with fixed periods of residence rather than simply to meet housing need.

Previously I have commented on the importance of being realistic and honest about your ability to affect the provision of services in the community. This is just as important when discussing probation resources and your own time and availability. There is a public image of the way we work, shared by magistrates and potential clients alike, that we see people once a week, every week. As I have pointed out above, that is just not possible, so I always try to emphasise this at the outset, so that people know what to expect. I explain that I have to visit 15 people in prisons, some of them a day's journey away, do court duty and supervise another 25 people. This usually comes as a considerable surprise, as clients generally imagine that they are one of between ten or twenty people selected for my special attention. If I get this in at the beginning it does not sound too much like an excuse, which it can do later on. When I have neglected to set all this out, people are surprised to see how little I contact them, and either think I have gone off them, their case is unimportant, or that I have decided to go easy on them.

## In conclusion

Most of this chapter has been a description of what happens during a probation or supervision order, in an attempt to lift some of the mists of secrecy with which we surround our work. Probation officers need to keep talking to each other about the way they actually work with clients to provide a realistic basis on which to develop their practice. There are pressures from the courts, management and the social work profession which we publicly acknowledge while privately at least partially ignoring them. If we can articulate a view of the work we actually do we may then be able to develop a theory which connects with and informs that work and enter into a constructive dialogue with these other bodies.

As well as discussing our practice with other probation officers, the other message of this chapter is the need to do the same with our clients. We know what controls and restrictions being on probation may involve, we know what we may or may not be able to do for someone. Our clients can only guess at all of this unless we spell it out for them. Not to do so can lead to frustration, disappointment, bewilderment or even unexpected imprisonment.

Finally, I return to my statement at the beginning of this chapter that one-to-one work during a probation order is a useful way of working, and a constructive alternative to custody. Offering an offender a year or two during which they will have someone to talk to (if they want), who may be able to help them with practical difficulties, is not going to make an enormous difference to the quality of their life. However, the difference it might make is well worth the effort, and the effect on their life will be far less destructive than a prison sentence. For these reasons alone I would argue that it is worth defending.

# 4

# Prison-based Work

Nigel Stone

This chapter will consider how socialist principles can guide practice in a way which is helpful to the lives and futures of prisoners, given the present realities of the prison system. Previous accounts have sought to demonstrate how social work in prisons can be creative against the odds, and that stress and ambiguity of role can be turned to effective advantage (Pratt, 1975; Smith, 1979). Little attempt has been made to develop a progressive framework for action, congruent with a radical analysis of the struggle for social justice. The issue has been both helpfully highlighted and simultaneously fudged by the debate within NAPO about the continued secondment of probation officers to work in penal establishments. However I do not wish to concentrate narrowly on that concern. My own view, argued elsewhere (Stone, 1982), is that NAPO policy favouring withdrawal from secondment is ultimately correct. I believe that the views presented here sustain and inform that conclusion and move beyond that debate, but also offer some pointers within the present division of labour.

More urgently, we need to defend and develop our work, however structured, as a social service to prisoners, in the face of current Home Office proposals:

> Sufficient resources should be allocated to through-care to enable the service's statutory obligations to be discharged ... Beyond that, social work for offenders released from custody, though important in itself, can only command the priority which is consistent with the main objective of implementing non-custodial measures. (Home Office, 1984, p.5)

This statement is ominous and could further weaken the already fragile nature of voluntary after-care. The Home

Office do not see after-care as making a sufficient contribution to their chosen priorities for the probation service – the prevention of offending and the enforcement of law (Stone, 1984). Even David Haxby's (1978, p.260) vision of a 'community correctional service' sees a justification for after-care as a straightforward social service which can act as 'a form of positive discrimination in favour of a group of clients who, as a result of their custodial experience, are socially disadvantaged and stigmatised'. The gap between vague and worthy rhetoric and actual service delivery has been a shaming default (Walker and Beaumont, 1981). This limited service is now being justified and rationalised in various management strategies, which anticipate the Home Office proposals and give reduced workload weighting and resources to after-care. We may be better able to resist this decline and relocate prison-based work as a central concern and commitment of the probation service if we re-examine the politics and function of imprisonment.

## An analysis of prison

Following a class-based analysis Mike Fitzgerald (1977, p.259) has starkly described imprisonment as 'one of the most visible symbols of the all-embracing hegemony established by the ruling class in a capitalist society'. Put more mildly: 'There is substantial evidence that the prison system contributes to division in society in that there is a differential liability between particlular social classes to suffer imprisonment at all; and if they do suffer it, to the ways in which they do so' (Morris, 1978, p.86). It is common wisdom to acknowledge the historical role of the prison 'to confine and discipline the poor, the unemployed, the unemployable, the socially disadvantaged and the socially inept' (Carlen, 1983a, p.209). Prison essentially draws its population from the unproductive working class, who are processed and recycled in a political climate of inertia, irresponsibility and ignorance. John McCarthy (1981, p.145), while a prison governor, described the persisting lack of change as a 'process of collusion, not only among those who work inside prisons but also between society and the prison system which maintains a "quiet society" by keeping trouble out of sight in a metaphorical dustbin'. Prisons thus embody the structural inequalities and injustices of society and the criminal justice system, and carry a self-perpetuating momentum. Their consequences – denial of autonomy, degradation of dignity, impairment of self-reliance, inculcation of authoritarian values, fracturing of family ties and stability and the reduction of prospects for economic or social improvement – are clear. Prisons are places where indecisiveness, favouritism, racism, sexism, suppression and lawlessness are daily played out, protected by secrecy, low visibility and the broad absence of due process of law.

One option suggested for radicals is that we leave well alone, to avoid any misleading impression of humanitarian innovation but clearly that is an unacceptably nihilistic stance. There is a tentative progressive consensus that we should seek to minimise the disadvantage gap between prisons/prisoners and society/citizens by reducing the apparatus of security, normalising the experience of custody, and establishing rights rather than privileges for prisoners. With the decline of a sham reformist ideology of imprisonment, and some modest but encouraging signs from the courts that they are prepared to break the 'hands off' rule in applying natural justice to prison issues, the notion of 'humane containment' as the guiding principle for imprisonment has gained considerable ground. Its constituent elements, laid out in NAPO's 1982 policy of support, based on Roy King and Rod Morgan's (1980) arguments, are:

That the aim and principle of imprisonment should be the humane containment of those for whom no other course of action is possible, and that, in particular, the following guidelines should be observed – (a)   that prisoners should generally be held in the establishment closest to their community ties so as to maximise their opportunity to maintain family and other links which are the norm for persons in the community; (b)   that prisoners should be permitted access to a similar range of health, welfare and educational facilities as they would have access to within the community; (c)   services within the prison should be provided by the same commercial, voluntary or statutory agencies which normally provide them within the community; (d)   that prisoners should be provided with a standard of accommodation (including normal services) food and clothing comparable to that provided by the State to persons in receipt of supplementary benefits; (e) that prisoners, wherever possible, should be afforded the opportunity of gainful employment thereby enabling them to improve their standard of living and to meet some of their community obligations; (f) that prison affairs should be freed from official secrets legislation; (g) that prisoners should be permitted to communicate on any matter with any persons or organisations that they choose, insofar as this does not make unreasonable demands upon staff time thereby prejudicing the welfare of other prisoners; (h) that all serious disciplinary offences should be subject to adjudication according to due process of law; (i) that all decisions which affect the date of a prisoner's release should be subject to judicial or some other independent form of review.

An integral adjunct to this policy is a considerable reduction of the prison population and the use of custody, achieved by the abolition of imprisonment as a sanction for various offences and defaults, reduction in the length of sentences and a bold use of the Home Secretary's powers of early release contained in Section 32 of the Criminal Justice Act 1982.

A considerable attraction of this approach is that rather than seeking to give imprisonment a vague 'positive' aim it recognises that imprisonment is the deprivation of liberty and provides yardsticks by which the humanity, fairness and dignity of that process can be measured for shortfall. Official endorsement of the policy of humane containment has been cautiously expressed by the then Director-General of the Prison Service (Trevelyan, 1982). Practical demonstration of such official policy is not forthcoming. There is a substantial risk that the nominal acceptance of the principle could lead to a further entrenchment of warehousing and containment, with a thin veneer of humanity. Laurie Taylor has warned that without safeguards:

> We will stay on the merry-go-round for another hundred years, having our doubts about the system periodically assuaged by a minor concession here and a little liberal handout there ... Without some action to change this state of affairs, we will continue to regard prisons ... as permanent institutional features of our society which occasionally need some internal reform instead of seeing ... the system of imprisonment for what it is – an institution more akin to slavery, a way of debasing and brutalising our fellow human beings which persistently undermines our claim to be a civilised society. (Taylor, 1978, p.205)

Another danger is that the only humane measures adopted may be those that suit prison officers:

> Humane containment tends to be confined to those improvements in conditions which make control easier, i.e. further the 'quiet life'. An example is the initial resistance of many staff to prisoners being allowed radios in their cells. This was seen as making life too comfortable for them. However, when it was realised that such inmates when locked up made less disturbance and rang their cell bells less often, the staff attitude changed. (McCarthy, 1981, p.151)

Neither are the benefits of humane containment guaranteed by formal support from official sources or liberal sympathisers. Geoff Coggan and Martin Walker (1982, p.115) have concluded:

> There are three crucial elements to the exposure of abuses inside prison: prisoners' collective action, the determination of the prisoner's family and external community support. Everything else – MPs questions, legal or 'civil liberties' intervention, the European Court of Human Rights, television documentaries – is peripheral and secondary. Constant burning pressure must be applied from elsewhere if any of these are to be stirred into effective action. Even then, in most cases, the heat must not be so strong as to risk fingers getting burnt.

The inspiration for a more radical approach to penal issues has been Thomas Mathiesen's *The Politics of Abolition* (1974), written in the light of his experience in the Norwegian prisoners' movement. This has been a major influence upon RAP and PROP. He tackles the problem of working for short-range reforms, introducing improvements into a system and simultaneously maintaining the long-range objective of abolishing that system, bearing in mind the risk that 'reforms of an improving kind may, by their very adjustments of, and relegitimation of, the prevailing order, actually lessen the possibilities of long-term abolition' (Mathieson, 1974, p.25). The priority, therefore, as RAP see it, is 'to gain support for the reforms of the penal system which, while making it more humane, will also show up its inherent limitations and contradictions' (Ward, 1982, p.22). Thomas Mathiesen (1974) develops a range of possibilities, short of abolition (working to do away with established systems you oppose):

*Defensive* – working to prevent new systems of the kind you are opposing from being established.

*Exposing*–unmasking the ideologies and myths which the punitive system relies on – so that real interests and actual conditions may be revealed.

*Negative reform*–changes which abolish or remove greater or smaller parts on which the system is more or less dependent.

These have been utilised by RAP to develop a new short-term strategy, such as seeking the end of censorship of prisoners' mail, solitary confinement, the prison medical service, and a number of changes which are close to 'humane containment' and 'rights' proposals. I now consider how these principles can be applied to the work of probation officers.

## Problems encountered in prison social work

Probation officers would claim that their contribution to-wards prisoners has always been firmly humanitarian. Thomas Mathiesen (1974, p.80) has described how subtly 'humanitarian work constitutes a way in which to "appear protesting" ', maintaining 'a kind of "criticism" ... which does not challenge the premises and rules of the establish-ment'. He warns how the pull in the direction of individual-ised humanitarian work tends to leave the structure over-shadowing prisoners unassailed. The shortfall and flaws in the official account of prison-based work have been exposed by Hilary Walker and Bill Beaumont (1981) and do not need to be repeated. I would suggest that to a considerable extent, probation officers have fulfilled Thomas Mathiesen's (1974, p.20) predictions about absorption:

*Incorporation*–the new is allowed only in a reduced form from the beginning.

*Initiation*–the rebel is initiated into the secrets of the system and is thereby brought to silence ... having received privileged communication.

*Responsibility*–you perform duties on the part of the system for which you are held responsible.

In many respects, prison social work suffers the same fate as prison medical work, as recognised by Dr MacKeith, formerly a medical officer at Brixton Prison: 'It is my impression that one of the most important roles for the medical officer from the Home Secretary's ... viewpoint is that his daily presence within the institution is taken as an unspoken comment that facilities are of an acceptable standard to the medical adviser' (in Coggan and Walker, 1982, p.217). In a similar way probation officers working in prisons give legitimacy to existing regimes.

The requirements on the seconded probation officer to be 'the normal channel of communication on social problems with the outside world' (Home Office, 1967) means that the needs of prisoners are not confronted as a central concern of institutional life, but are unnecessarily diverted through a 'welfare filter'. In this way help with problems becomes an uneven and uncertain privilege rather than a routine expectation. This channelling may have institutional advantages in sustaining surveillance and the quiet 'nick', but what might be regarded as natural and straightforward facilities become laborious and intermittent extras, subject to delay, dependency, discretion and failure to deliver.

The channel of communication is substantially hampered by the Official Secrets Acts, by which seconded officers are explicitly bound, and which have elastic effects of a strongly inhibiting nature. As Geoff Coggan and Martin Walker (1982, p.222) point out, 'the prison welfare service shows clearly what happens when a professional body is subordinated to the prison disciplinary structure'. They refer to the impotence of prison-based officers in the face of institutional abuse such as the events in Wormwood Scrubs D Wing in 1979. At a more routine level, there have recently been a number of disciplinary steps taken against probation officers and other similarly placed professional workers such as teachers and chaplains, for breach of the prison rule that staff are not allowed to associate with discharged prisoners unless approved by the governor; a prohibition which cuts considerably the scope for resettlement work. This vulnerability was further demonstrated by my own exclusion from a prison for communicating to a prisoner's solicitor about a matter involving internal discipline and the prisoner's mental state. Although potentially embarrassing to staff, this was not a breach of institutional confidentiality, and could have been conveyed by the prisoner himself. The reaction was a variation on that familiar protective device in institutions, the 'no grassing' rule.

Additionally, probation officers operate their own version of negative discrimination towards prisoners:

> A recent study ... of the priorities used by probation officers in managing their workload shows that they regard after-care cases as lower priority than probation or social enquiry cases; and that voluntary after-care was rated as less important than statutory licence supervision ... and, if valid, would point to the conclusion that one of the disadvantages consequent upon imprisonment was a second class service from probation officers. (Corden, 1983, p.84)

We thus collude with the convenient opportunity imprisonment provides for personal problems and social injustice to be 'cooled out' – removed from public scrutiny and discomfort in the court room, postponed and later processed quietly out through the prison gate, when difficulties are likely to be more severe as a result of sentence. The weakness and inconsistency of our work in the resettlement of ex-offenders has been further convincingly exposed in a recent report, which concluded that none of the efforts surveyed amounted to a co-ordinated strategy for resettlement (NACRO, 1983a).

We need to shape progressive, radical and congruent practice, recognising the nature of the power structure and our marginality, enjoying access without incorporation, and acknowledging the need for care in choosing what and when to confront. We need to utilise the modest room for manoeuvre available to us to achieve extensions of humanity and rights, and to raise an abolitionist challenge so that, as Thomas Mathiesen (1980, p.237) says, the response naturally arises: 'Yes, but as far as I can see this presupposes a much more sweeping change.'

**The potential for practice**

The role of the probation service in relation to institutions which seem systematically designed to make individuals maladjusted should have two broad aims:

*Survival Help.* In the community we are accustomed to being alongside individuals in their effort to negotiate with agencies, institutions and officialdom and helping them make best use of their opportunities and attachments. Work in prison should be essentially no different, albeit in an artificial and all-embracing environment. Our capacity to inform, advise, interpret and mediate should be amplified to sustain and enhance the prisoner's capacity to cope and utilise opportunities. This should help to combat the sense of powerlessness, dependency and erosion of initiative. This encompasses helping prisoners to deal with feelings and emotions generated by their experience of imprisonment. We may be the only trustworthy, non-partisan, accessible outsiders available.

*Sustaining an Outside Identity.* This means helping prisoners to maintain their community ties, rights, responsibilities and affiliations as far as is possibly compatible with loss of liberty.

We are thus required to be outsiders with intimate 'inside' knowledge and the capacity to interpret the two worlds to each other, with their difference of priorities, sense of time and expectations. Within these broad aims, areas for particular attention and expansion include the following key issues.

*Free access and communication*

Prisoners should have as full access to, and communication with, community facilities, advice services and agencies as they would outside, compatible with minimum necessary demands of security. This places the probation service in perspective as an obvious community resource which should be readily available to prisoners. Simultaneously we should be helping prisoners to seek access to other relevant organisations which may offer pertinent services, and supporting those agencies in gaining routine and regular access to prisons. These include the Marriage Guidance Council, which has a reasonable presence in some prisons, and the Samaritans, who have encountered greater difficulty in becoming accessible to prisoners, other than on certain pre-release courses. Given the incidence of suicidal behaviour among prisoners, this opportunity is overdue as a humane facility. A useful pilot project is the Winson Green Prison Housing Advice Centre which NACRO has developed, and hopes to extend to other prisons to assist with accommodation issues (NACRO, 1983a). Prisoners have inadequate access to legal services and we may be able to promote legal advice 'surgeries' which would be an important resource.

The prevailing trend is not so encouraging. Access to lawyers is readily hampered, particularly for remand prisoners, either because of the complexities of remand allocation such as in the London prison system, or because of staff rostering problems such as in Bristol Prison. Furthermore, new initiatives to provide legal advice for prisoners have been delayed. For instance, at Wandsworth Prison a proposal for a legal advice project inside the prison was turned down in 1983.

Probation officers should ensure that prisoners are receiving basic access to services as permitted by present rules, and attempt to foster new links and resources of the kind described. As a necessary adjunct to resources, there should be adequate facilities and privacy for contact. The uncomplaining tolerance of both probation officers and prisoners in submitting to 'confidential' interviews in crowded visiting areas has done little to extend the case for decent facilities as of right.

### Better information

We can contribute to prisoners' access to and awareness of the rules regulating their predicament by putting our own house in order as regards the prisoners' knowledge of the probation system and resources (how many prisoners can readily lay hands on a Probation Directory?). We could acquire greater access to and familiarity with prison regulations and standing orders (many of which are 'secret' and difficult to get hold of), help prisoners to understand these rules and make use of the protection they may provide. We should help prisoners to grasp the range and whereabouts of community resources which may be of use to them. These will include voluntary bodies which specialise in particular needs and interests of prisoners, such as the Black Prisoners' Welfare Scheme, the Help Asian Prisoners Group (still seeking Home Office approval to distribute to Asians in custody information about its work) and Women in Prison.

### Due process and fairness

Prisoners should have access to files and records relating to them, except those explicitly relating to security. We should be able to set standards and expectations with regard to our own records, and this will help to counteract the mystification of the process and the frequent gratuitous denial of adult status. This has particular importance in the vital area of decision making about release under parole or home leave, to which probation officers are requested to provide information and opinion. While we are not able to transform the legal basis of such decisions, we could place this work on a near-identical footing to social enquiry report preparation. Good practice requires an active partnership with an individual, to examine the circumstances and proposals pertinent to the issue for decision, and then sets out the chances of the measure succeeding.

There should, as NAPO (1983a) suggests, be one probation presentation to the parole assessment, prepared by the community-based probation officer in consultation with the prison-based officer. Practice in parole requires close scrutiny to highlight the frequent unjustified departures from fairness by report writers:

● in writing reports on individuals they have never met;
● in offering opinions on matters on which they are not competent to judge. For example: 'It would be clearly irresponsible to release him at this stage' and 'In view of

rumours circulating of people wishing to settle old scores with the prisoner, I cannot recommend parole because of the "degree of risk" ';
● in making untoward moral judgements, or predictions based on 'treatment' grounds or an unduly rehabilitative notion of parole. For example: 'He has not taken up offers of voluntary contact and has in the past sought to use the probation service for his own ends' and 'He won't avail himself of the opportunity for effective counselling';
● in not giving the subject of the report the chance to see and respond to reports.

It is not surprising that the prisoner seeking parole can feel like a unit to be investigated rather than a person to be helped.

*Family attachments*

An important requirement for the benefit of prisoners and their families is that sentence should be served in the locality of normal residence. This principle and a range of allied proposals which would sustain and enhance family life despite imprisonment are outlined in the recent NACRO report *Forgotten Victims: How Prison affects the Family* (1983b), and have been argued for persistently by organisations such as the Prisoners' Wives Service. Practitioners need to challenge the complacency which has allowed the status quo to persist:

● by arguing repeatedly the case for transfer and the consequences of separation;
● by pressurising for financial help for families on low incomes to make a second monthly visit;
● by complaining about uncomfortable, undignified visiting facilities, which allow neither privacy nor adequate time.

We should be better informed than any other organisation to comment on the consequences of the present short-fall. Such challenges, argued on the basis of the immediate and the individual, beg far larger questions about the allocation system, the excessive use of security, and the location of prisons.

Again, there are obstacles to innovation. In 1978 a planned facility at Styal for extended family visits, using caravans within the prison perimeter, was blocked by staff objections. In 1980, an experiment allowing prisoners at Kirkham Open Prison the use of pay 'phones was discontinued because of POA objections (NACRO, 1983b).

*Community resources*

NACRO points out that, aside from pre-release courses (a favourite new initiative for prison-based probation officers) which reach only a minority of prisoners, there is 'little evidence of much co-ordinated effort at present to provide practical information about housing, jobs, money and relationships' (NACRO, 1983a, p.31). The report refers to a survey in Channings Wood Prison which revealed that prisoners wanted help with employment, accommodation, income tax and supplementary benefit, making money last, and family responsibilities and parenthood; 'many of these subjects requiring specialist knowledge and experience which it would be unrealistic to expect a probation officer to have and impractical for him or her to set about acquiring' (NACRO, 1983a, p.30). There is an obvious role for the service to act as convenor of resettlement services to prisoners and ex-prisoners. NACRO's proposal is for community resettlement units in every large urban area, to bring together expertise, co-ordinate existing provision and to identify new areas for development – 'they would ensure that existing resources are better used; the system is more coherent for those who have to work it and use it, and more people are permanently settled into the community' (NACRO, 1983a, p.41).

This focus might at least offer the prospect of a more systematic review of the relevance and uptake of services. Modest but encouraging possibilities are suggested by the Bedfordshire Education Through-Care Project, run by Bedfordshire Probation Service, which has enabled up to 20 per cent of ex-prisoners returning to the county to take an educational course on release (NACRO, 1983a,). Education for serving prisoners has received little encouragement from a recent government statement, which declined the proposal of the All Party Select Committee on Education, Science and Arts for a statutory right to education during imprisonment (HMSO, 1984). Such a proposal would have been a major initiative in normalising the lives of prisoners, comparative to other citizens. Whether it be in respect of education, housing or retraining, the needs of ex-prisoners have to be faced more responsibly by the agencies which provide them in the community. Prisoners might then for instance stand a better chance of being integrated into accommodation opportunities appropriate for adults seeking independence and self-determination than at present. Many facilities now available to ex-prisoners and promoted by probation officers are unduly paternalistic and continue the dependency of the institution.

Local authorities face a particular challenge. One way of increasing their role and responsibility, so far only tentatively attempted, is for councils to forge links with local prisons, for example by being represented on Boards of Visitors. This would have the vital advantage of making prisons more accountable to the local community and less insular and remote. Such initiatives could be promoted by probation officers working through local political parties.

*Multiple disadvantage*

NACRO has called attention to the 'additional special intermediate help needed if discharged prisoners are to use community facilities' (NACRO, 1983a, p.20). This is especially true for those labelled 'persistent, petty offenders', over whom there is much hand-wringing about the obvious need to divert them from the prison system, but who end up receiving the least service. John Corden (1983) has characterised such people as balls in a depressing pinball machine who ricochet between associated disadvantages in income, housing and employment, alcohol dependence, social isolation and increased probability of further court appearances and prison sentences. His study of prisoners on release in West Yorkshire suggests that these individuals generally have the least expectations of after-care and least contact with the probation service.

Such prisoners tend to be obliged to cross the great divide between the inside world and the community alone, and experience the usual hiatus on release before help and support is mobilised. Their problems, generally made more critical as a result of imprisonment make them amongst the severest casualties of the criminal justice system. These prisoners demand much higher priority, contrary to probation area restrictions such as withdrawing from work with prisoners serving less than six months. We need to understand more clearly the patterns of disadvantage and ways of breaking the cycle. John Corden (1983) comments that isolated attempts to break one link in the cycle are unlikely to succeed and suggests checklists both for use in identifying needs, and as the criteria against which to check local resources.

## Self-help

There has been discussion among socialist writers about establishing 'popular' and localised justice systems in place of judicial criminal justice. Ian Taylor (1981) has suggested democratisation within the prison system, and democratic assemblies of prisoners and prison officers. This has been correctly dismissed by RAP as blindness to the 'inherently anti-democratic and anti-egalitarian nature of imprisonment (Box-Grainger, 1982a, p.18). More realistic self-help developments might involve encouraging prisoners and ex-prisoners to maximise opportunities available to help themselves and each other. This is obviously going on all the time, but it may be possible to enhance the capacity of individuals to give sustained support and advice. For example, a prisoner with whom I dealt was able to help new prisoners from his home area in making sense of their families' social security and related problems, because of his own struggle to achieve welfare rights.

Self-help has necessarily been a slow and limited development for ex-prisoners who are obviously not as inclined to acknowledge such an identity as other need groups. The major success in achieving a campaigning voice for prisoners has been PROP, the National Prisoners' Movement. PROP has been through a painful process of adjustment in seeking to find a consistent identity which does not mislead prisoners or lose all credibility. It has now achieved a maturity of purpose and established itself as a persuasive campaigning pressure group, particularly in marshalling legal action and in identifying prison abuses of human rights. It needs support from probation officers to become more accessible to prisoners, together with information which can enhance its arguments. Many prisoners will be aware that there are few opportunities open to them to seek redress by legitimate means. We may be able to direct them to constructive channels such as Justice, and the (albeit restricted) use that can be made of the Ombudsman in regard to prison maladministration (Wener, 1983).

A most heartening example of self-help has emerged in the North London Baggshott group, a pioneering, self-supporting housing and work co-operative. Set up by ex-prisoners, for ex-prisoners, in democratic manner without funding or patronage, and independent of 'helping agencies', it seeks to offer members ideas for regaining control of their lives without crime, by using personal and collective resources and opportunities in the local community (Winfield and Riddick, 1983, p.20). It is bound to be difficult but is vital for such collectives to make and receive direct contact with serving prisoners, despite the ex-con status which usually forecloses such contacts. Probation officers may be able to support this communication, which will need to be argued for in each prison establishment where it is sought, because of widespread local discretion. As the demand for such co-operatives increases (and Baggshott are keen to offer support and advice to others) then officers may be able to help in promoting this approach without seeking to colonise its potential.

In more modest ways, it may be possible to develop new approaches to after-care which do not carry the paternalistic connotations which prisoners experience as invasions of their liberty. The housing options available for homeless prisoners often demand considerable sacrifice of autonomy and disposable income, and we often seem to be squeezing the individual into an ill-fitting resource. In an attempt to counter this, in partnership with an ex-prisoner who had the original idea, I have been able to obtain property from a local authority for accommodation for ex-prisoners. They take responsibility for the running of the house without supervision, supporting each other and pooling their resources and income.

### Campaigning and making alliances

The service is uniquely placed to have a window on the prison world, and to comment on the misuses and abuses of custody. We have not distinguished ourselves by speaking out when prisoners, individually or collectively, are disadvantaged, or where imprisonment is used inappropriately. One example of status discrimination about which a NAPO branch has campaigned is the unfair position of prisoners transferred out to mental hospitals compared with compulsorily detained civil patients (Kemp, 1983). This report also called for proper mental health treatment within the NHS for prisoners who develop mental illness, and an end to solitary confinement within the penal system as a means of behaviour modification or punishment. An example of work on the inappropriate use of custody is the research done by probation officers at Whatton Detention Centre about the previous convictions of trainees and the limited use of non-custodial measures prior to sentence (Thomas, 1982).

Campaigns may need to be mounted to resist unacceptable developments and strategies in the prison system. Thus when the government's response in 1980 to reasonable industrial action by the POA was to set up army-manned temporary prisons, there was clear scope, had the action continued, for probation officers to refuse as a union to service such establishments. This would have been an opportunity to show solidarity with another union within the prison system. Our general stance will obviously challenge at times the policies and behaviour of other prisons workers, as in seeking to identify and counteract racism in penal establishments. But we must also be alert to possible alliances with fellow workers on particular issues, as well as with other campaigning organisations.

Campaigning has to be handled tactically to maximise impact and protect the vulnerability of individuals, both prisoners and workers. This is not a healthy season for moles, and the prison system has solid protective mechanisms. However, an example of useful, important, small-scale work has been the identification of prisoners who were unfairly and adversely affected by the changes in parole and life sentence policy, announced in 1983, which had led to retrospective recategorisation of people anticipating early release.

## In conclusion

The suggestions made here for action and practice are certainly not of a high order of major radical change, though they lead logically to placing ourselves clearly and unambiguously as an outside community-based service. They are intended to be appropriately modest and reachable targets given the massive blocks in the path of change, our marginal position within the criminal justice system, and our need to retain some acceptance within prisons. Nevertheless I hope that they expand the rights of prisoners and increase the humanity of the system whilst linked, at least implicitly, to broader abolitionist policy. We need to develop our capacity to act as grit in an otherwise complacent system, to be respected for that, to help prisoners increase their self-awareness of their social world, and to achieve some reduction in the deviant scapegoat role which prisoners carry.

We should seek to counteract the deformation of individuals and assert the dignity, worth and responsibility of prisoners, without seeking to sustain the legitimacy of imprisonment. At the same time, we need to oppose the tendency towards prejudged fatalism about the prospects for many of the most disadvantaged prisoners, and to re-evaluate continually the breakdown of resettlement bids. We may thus be able to retain 'after-care' as a primary and growing focus of the service and practice Thomas Mathiesen's art of the 'unfinished', into the uncertain future.

# 5

# Women's Issues in Probation Practice

Hilary Walker

This chapter relates thinking which has emerged from the women's movement to some areas of probation work, with an emphasis on its implications for practice. A fundamental challenge has been posed to our traditional understanding of the role and position of women. In this welfare capitalist society women are viewed as subordinate to men; this attitude is justified by attributing a set of characteristics to women solely on the basis of their sex. These stereotypical views of women as invisible (subsumed in 'he' and 'men'), dependent on men, ruled by their biology, confined to the home, as mothers and sex objects, have now been challenged. As significant as the thinking itself is the way in which it developed. Women met together and shared their personal, material and emotional experiences; from this emerged a political understanding of their oppression. The analysis thus synthesises the personal and the political, providing new, radical ways of approaching issues. For instance, women's experiences of marital difficulties can no longer simply be explained in terms of personal problems but also as a consequence of the power differential in marriage. Social work and probation work, along with other state institutions, have implicitly accepted a view of women as subordinate and have been slow in responding to the challenges of feminist thinking. The probation service, which employs more male than female probation officers and is concerned predominantly with male clients, shows signs of resistance at both formal and informal levels.

In this book we seek to make connections between practice

and the analytical base outlined in *Probation Work* (Walker and Beaumont, 1981). However in considering women's issues we encounter a theoretical problem which deserves mention. Our analysis in *Probation Work* was essentially class based, and did not address itself sufficiently to the oppression of women as a group nor to the dimension of sex within a class analysis. This problem, to which there appears to be no satisfactory resolution, is shared with other commentators (Wilson, 1980; Smart, 1981). Tension surrounding this theoretical issue will run through this chapter since, while a class analysis of society does not fully explain women's oppression, neither is assigning women to a single class satisfactory (Wilson, 1980).

The concerns of probation are, in a sense, justifiably male-oriented, for offences are predominantly committed by men. Of offenders sentenced in England and Wales in 1982, 88 per cent were men and only 12 per cent women (Home Office, 1983b). Unsurprisingly, therefore, criminology and deviancy studies have been male dominated. Other concerns of probation supervision – work and its corollary, earned leisure (Walker and Beaumont, 1981) – are intimately connected to the traditional stereotype of male identity (Tolson, 1977). They have limited relevance to women who are not assumed to be wage earners and whose unpaid labour in the home makes the division between work and leisure unclear. Although men will continue to be the main focus of probation work, there are important insights from feminist thinking which should provoke a re-assessment of practice with both men and women. Three main areas will be considered here: women in the criminal justice system; male crimes against women; and issues concerning women in relation to male clients. Space precludes consideration of other important issues such as equality of opportunity, sexual harassment, child-care and matrimonial work. This chapter seeks to begin an overdue exploration of a practice perspective consistent with the rejection of sexism.

## Women in the criminal justice system

Women's involvement in crime is a difficult area, more beset with pitfalls than most criminal statistics. It is probably safe to conclude that female crime is still a small problem despite relative increases in recent years. As women become more visible generally, there is a danger of female crime being given disproportionate attention and of a moral panic developing (Morris and Gelsthorpe, 1981). Numbers of female probation clients are relatively small and most probation officers will have few on their caseloads. This may reinforce the tendency to deal with women clients as exceptional or abnormal rather than reaching for a broader understanding from studies of female offenders and shared information within the team. The assumption that women are treated with paternal benevolence within the criminal justice system is now open to question (Smart, 1976; Mawby, 1977; NACRO, 1978a). For example, it is assumed that having children protects women from being sent to prison, yet over 1000 children have mothers in custody (NACRO, 1981). Indeed women may be dealt with more harshly if thought to be 'sheltering' behind their children. A woman judge told two defendants:

> I have no doubt that you have brought your babies to court in order to try and blackmail me. All I can say is that when I see you in three weeks time you had better not bring the babies. I do not care if you bring a whole host of babies – a whole orphanage – because it is not going to stop me from sending you to Borstal or prison if necessary. (*South London Press*, 1 February 1980)

Later, describing them as 'brazen hussies', she sentenced one to prison and the other to borstal.

Other features in the sentencing of women disrupt the assumption of leniency. A higher proportion of women *remanded in custody* are not eventually sentenced to imprisonment than is the case for men (Mawby, 1977). In 1982, 73 per cent of the 3598 women remanded in custody were found not guilty or given non-custodial sentences (NACRO, 1983c). Since remands are very disruptive for those women who bear responsibility for home and children, this high use must be seen as punitive. In 1982, 1324 women were received into prison for *fine default*; 31 per cent of women sentenced compared to 26 per cent of sentenced men (Home Office, 1983c). This too is punitive when women's material circumstances are appreciated. They are far less likely to have the independent means to pay fines; they may rely on state benefits or a man's income and his discretion about whether or not to hand it over. A greater proportion of women than men are serving sentences for relatively *minor offences* such as theft, handling, fraud and forgery – 43 per cent of women prisoners compared to 23 per cent of men at 30 June 1982 (Home Office, 1983b). Indeed many women are serving short sentences for those less serious crimes where the use of prison is most questionable.

Women are proportionately more likely to be placed *on probation* than men; in 1982 they made up 12 per cent of those sentenced by the courts, but 30 per cent of those placed on probation. For each offence for which reliable statistics are available women are more likely than men to be placed on probation (Home Office, 1983b). This does not necessarily indicate more lenient treatment; they may be put on probation because they are unable to pay fines, or be considered in need of help simply because they are women offenders. Women are proportionately less likely to be sentenced to *community service* than men. In 1982 only 5 per cent of those sentenced to community service were women (Home Office, 1983b). An analysis of 100 social enquiry reports prepared on offenders committed for sentence to a London crown court in 1981 showed that almost 9 per cent of men had community service orders recommended, compared to just over 1 per cent of women (Mitra, 1983). This alternative to imprisonment appears to be less available to women because of their domestic responsibilities:

> In our opinion we would have great difficulty in placing Miss X. She has a young child of 4 months and she insists the child would have to accompany her on the community service project. Obviously because of the needs of a young child the amount of actual community service she could do would be minimal. (Extract from a community service report)

In their recent study David Farrington and Allison Morris (1983, p.243), testing the view that men are more harshly sentenced than women, concluded that 'the major reason why men appeared to be sentenced more severely than women was not because of their sex but because they tended to commit more serious offences'. While research evidence is not conclusive it is clear that women are treated differently within the criminal justice system and that this is probably not to their advantage.

*Sentencing by stereotype*   Research shows that women are far more likely than men to be processed in court on an assessment of their personal circumstances. Pat Carlen (1983b) points out that sheriffs, when faced with a sentencing dilemma, were likely to decide the sentence according to a judgement of the woman as a mother. David Farrington and Allison Morris found the most important predictor of sentence to be type of offence but that other factors related to sentence severity were different for men and women:

> Women convicted with one or more other offenders were more likely to receive severe sentences than those convicted alone... Women who were in the 'other' category of marital status (predominantly divorced or separated rather than widowed) received relatively severe sentences as did women coming from a deviant family background (coming from a broken home usually). (Farrington and Morris, 1983, p.245)

This suggests that within the criminal justice system, role expectations of women and the stereotypes that operate will influence their treatment. There are several strong stereotypes of the woman offender which, as Victoria Greenwood (1982) has pointed out, are not mutually exclusive but merge and diverge providing contrary and confusing pictures.

A powerful stereotype is that of the female offender as *unbalanced or mad.* Criminological theories have tended to explain women's deviancy by reference to unfounded assertions about their 'true' characteristics of irrationality and neuroticism (Smart, 1976). The Central Council of Probation Committees (1981, p.8) asserts: 'The average woman under supervision by probation staff seems to be more unstable and demanding than her male counterpart.' Such views influence the treatment of women within the criminal justice system. The rebuilt Holloway Prison was intended to provide medical/psychiatric assessment and treatment for remand and sentenced female prisoners (RAP, 1972). Women are disproportionately remanded in custody for medical reports after conviction; in 1982 they accounted for 7 per cent of all unsentenced prisoners, but 18 per cent of those remanded for medical reports (Home Office, 1983c). Women are often characterised as being *at the mercy of their anatomy and emotions*. Most studies of female offenders 'refer to women in terms of their biological impulses and hormonal balance or in terms of their domesticity, maternal instinct and passivity' (Smart, 1976, p.xiv). The Central Council of Probation Committees (1981) describes female offenders thus; 'All are highly emotional: frequently they present major problems of depression, alcoholism and drug abuse' (p.3) and talks of 'the irrational jealousies of which women are capable' (p.7).

Since criminal behaviour is thought to contradict the idealised female role, women offenders are often characterised as *evil*. This theme is popular with the media which glory in headlines such as 'Sugar Daddy Killer' and 'Crime Orgy of Blonde and Bank Robber'. The logical consequence of this stereotype is harsh treatment for female offenders such as the Conservative proposal that 'military style, short, sharp prison sentences' should be extended to girls (*Guardian*, 25 May 1982). *Women's sexuality* is held against them within the criminal justice system. Maggie Casburn's study of juvenile justice demonstrated that girls appearing before the court had their sexual behaviour investigated and commented on but boys did not. She points out 'our code of sexual mores incorporates a double standard of morality–promiscuity in men equates with masculinity, yet we dub the promiscuous female "slut", "slag" and "scrubber"' (Casburn, 1979, p.14). In the same way prostitutes are regularly prosecuted for soliciting, while kerb crawling is rarely defined as illegal.

Despite these pervasive operational stereotypes it is clear that most women caught up in the criminal justice system are 'depressingly normal' (Heidenson, 1981, p.129); 'ordinary women, overstrained and debilitated by the exigencies of life' (Greenwood, 1982). However it has been argued that women may sometimes find the use of stereotypes to their benefit. Anne Worrall (1981) shows that if the image of the woman defendant suggests that she is out of place in court, then she may be treated with leniency, with paternal benevolence. Probation officers are not immune from attitudes held in general society. Sue Whitlock, writing about running a women's group in probation, provides some insights into probation officers' attitudes. She describes the difficulties of discussing the group with male colleagues who:

> tolerated our views, but suggested nothing to change the system in terms of the traditional view of female offenders, particularly regarding the pervasive stereotypes attached to women living on our team patch, who were frequently seen as bad wives, poor home managers, inadequate mothers or simply amoral. (Whitlock, 1983, p.12)

## *Points for practice*

Probation officers must *reassess their attitudes to women* in general and thus to women offenders. They should challenge the stereotypes applied to women in their personal practice and in team discussion. Attitudes towards double standards applied must be critically examined. For instance, behaviour that is criticised in women but not in men – sexual behaviour, assertiveness, independence – must be re-evaluated in an acceptance of women's rights. Probation officers must recognise the real material difficulties faced by women – the double shift of working inside and outside the home, poverty, dependence, heavy family responsibilities and oppressive relationships. If all these factors are carried into probation practice, it should transform work with women.

The treatment of women in court has been highlighted as an area where women may suffer discrimination. So probation officers need to *examine carefully their social enquiry reports* on women because of their contribution not only to sentencing but also to the forming of opinions by the bench. It will be necessary to be wary about using stereotypes; in principle it seems correct to avoid their use. However since it has been suggested that their use may lead to leniency (Worrall, 1981) probation officers may choose to use them tactically, thus perpetuating them. Perhaps a way ahead is to offer more choice to women about their presentation in court reports, to share with them the strategic possibilities and allow them to join in these decisions. It is important to remember the general picture of women's treatment in the courts when preparing a report on an individual so as to counterbalance prevailing trends. Reports must also be informed by the structural oppression and practical difficulties facing women; for instance the problems they face in paying fines. Team discussion of reports and recommendations could help to establish a more general picture of women offenders and reduce the danger of their being treated as abnormal.

Attention must also be given to both the level and type of *provision for women* within the criminal justice system. This means actively planning for women rather than assuming they can slot into the facilities already available for men. Provision must not be limited by the traditional view that women should be confined to domesticity and the home. It should instead be aiming to provide opportunities for women to extend their prospects in the community through education and training; groups, day centres and hostels should adopt this aim.

Probation officers should be working to rectify the exclusion of women from non-custodial measures because of their domestic responsibilities. The provision of creche facilities or baby-sitters would enable women with children to do community service or attend day centres. It may be necessary to make determined efforts to modify the male-oriented culture of day centres to encourage women to attend, or for women-only days to be allocated. Finally, women should be able to choose to be supervised by a female probation officer or attend an all-woman group. It is sometimes necessary for women to exclude men in order to create the environment where they can talk freely 'about their personal experiences of stereotyping in relation to the police, the courts and the judiciary (all male dominated) as well as at the hands – sadly often literally – of their menfolk' (Whitlock, 1983, p.12).

## Male crimes against women

The purpose of this section is to take a fresh look at those (men) who commit crimes of assault, rape, incest and indecent assault against women and children. Alternative explanations for these crimes will be considered and the implications of such thinking for probation officers and their male clients discussed. The issues raised are sensitive and may pose fundamental problems for probation officers, such as the conflict between protection of the victim and the welfare of clients. Probation officers need to consider their attitudes to such crimes, since these will directly influence their views on causation, the offender, the role of the victim and what should be done. For example, until recently, the Freudian psychoanalytic perspective has implicitly or explicitly been adopted by professionals in dealing with violence against wives. Because it reinforces conventional wisdom about relationships between men and women, it has upheld the view that the wife encourages, provokes or even enjoys abusive treatment (Dobash and Dobash, 1979). Attention has recently been drawn to these crimes as previously unacknowledged victims, supported by the women's movement, have begun to articulate their experiences (Smart, 1976). Alternative analyses with important implications have been developed. Convincing evidence of physical and psychological damage inflicted as a result of these crimes has been produced by Women's Aid, Incest Survivors and Rape Crisis centres. Such criminal behaviour should be understood in terms of the general male domination of women and specifically the power relationship of husband over wife or father over child. An important aspect of this dominance is the man's 'right' to enforce his will on his wife, child or rape victim. A key issue is that victims of such crimes should not be held responsible as has been common practice: 'Whether it is a rape, a murder or a beating, the victim's "part" or "role" in the incident is always a subject of debate' (Seddon, 1981, p.15).

Research and evidence reveal that, contrary to assumptions, rape is often planned, committed by men who know their victim and takes place in the victim's home. Many rape victims do not fit the stereotype of the sexually attractive or alluring female and indeed they include pregnant and elderly women; thus rape cannot be understood as an erotic act. Among men convicted of rape there is no strong indication of sexual abnormality; it is not the result of uncontrollable biological urges. Rather it tends to be a man forcing his will on a woman in an act of aggression, hatred, humiliation and degradation (Smart and Smart, 1978; Seddon, 1981). The vast majority of incest cases known to the police involve father and daughter. Sarah Nelson (1982, p.10) points out that when incest takes place it tends to be in families where 'traditional beliefs about the roles of husband, wife and daughter are taken to extremes: when the family members are seen as the husband's property and sex is among the services they are expected to provide'. She also explains the meaning of incest for the victim: 'From . . . accounts, several points emerge repeatedly: active initiation by the father; his use of force or authority to gain compliance; the girl's ignorance about sex, and her confusion about what is happening; her shame, fear or terror; and lack of pleasure in the act' (p.36).

By far the most common of these crimes is wife-beating. This act, often not taken seriously as a crime, is connected to the subordinate position of women within marriage and the family and to the 'right of men to dominate their wives by various means including force' (Dobash and Dobash, 1979, p.234). The evidence of women beaten, kicked and scalded in their own houses by their menfolk confirms the assertion that 'the resort to violence as a way of resolving difficulties is a physical manifestation of power, of the insistence of using all the methods available to you to achieve your ends' (Seddon, 1981, p.15).

The accumulated evidence suggests that such crimes must be taken more seriously. One danger of this is that it may feed into the retributive, savage sentencing lobby (Box-Grainger, 1982b). This poses a contradiction for those holding progressive views on criminal justice policy who in general argue for leniency, lesser sentences and decriminalisation for some offences. This will include probation officers who tend to adopt a position of unequivocal concern for the offender. They face difficult problems, for instance, over what to recommend in their reports on men convicted of rape or incest. Elizabeth Wilson (1983, p.224) advocates a long-term educative approach: 'The *priority* for all progressives must be to change attitudes, not to fight over what to do about individual men.' Nevertheless probation officers need to find immediate, practical and realistic ways of dealing with individual male offenders.

*Points for practice*
Probation officers have to date paid little attention to *wider general provision for women*, neither is it prominent on the NAPO agenda. In order to assist and support the (women) victims of these crimes, demands for more women's refuges, rape crisis centres, changes in the tax and social security laws, better work, education and training opportunities, decent child-care provision, access to abortion and to women-centred health facilities should be supported. For as Elizabeth Wilson (1983, p.223) writes 'it is obvious that no woman is free from the threat of violence unless she has an adequate income for herself and her children, if any, and independent access to shelter'.

Probation officers must be prepared to *re-assess their attitude to the family* and their general priority that families should be kept together. The analyses of incest and wife assault show that the roots of such crimes lie in the institution of the family and its power relationships. Probation officers need to be alert to the danger that their practice implicitly supports oppressive relationships within the family. They must search for the correct balance between legitimate concern for the offender, including his need for accommodation, and the protection of victims. Probation officers will need to find constructive ways of dealing with these issues; in some cases *probation hostels* may represent a way forward. In the instances of incest and wife-assault, exclusion from the home is often appropriate in order to protect the victim and allow other members of the family an opportunity to reassess their feelings and make decisions about the future. In the long term the family may be re-united. Probation hostels could be used as places of temporary residence allowing relevant work with both the offender and the family. Rebecca and Russell Dobash (1979, p.238) point out, for example, in the instance of violence against wives that 'some men, especially those who have not been married very long, will feel repentant about their use of violence and may seriously desire to change; their feelings provide a useful starting point for working with the family'. As caring professionals, probation officers cannot afford to dismiss these men. They must be prepared to give the offender another chance – others including his wife and children may not be prepared to do so. However the style of work carried out is important; probation officers need to point out that such behaviour is unacceptable and work towards change in attitudes and beliefs. *New ways of working* with these men must be pioneered. Male probation officers have a central responsibility here to engage with clients in the task of challenging and reassessing values and beliefs about male and female roles and sexuality. They will need to prepare to undertake this work by examining their own attitudes in discussion with women. However were they to talk openly with clients about their experience of attitude change, it could help to overcome some of the problems of client resistance.

The analysis presented here will have *implications for some methods of working*. For instance, conciliation, currently gaining status and popularity, may need reassessment. The method is based on the view of a couple as equal partners who can meet face to face in the presence of a probation officer in order constructively to resolve issues in the break-up of their marriage, such as custody and access. The analysis of marriage as a power relationship in which women are subordinate presented here contradicts the central assumption of conciliation work. The implications of this analysis need to be incorporated into the model of conciliation. In particular, the issue of violence experienced by women in marriage needs careful consideration. If a woman is seeking divorce because of assaults on her by her husband, it must be questionable whether it is appropriate to expect her to go through this process of conciliation.

It is fruitless to work towards radical ways of dealing with these offenders without recognising the oppressive way in which women are viewed in society generally, for this has an impact on the way in which both male offenders and male probation officers think and behave. Women live daily with sexism, sexist jokes and innuendo. The media present them as 'whores' or 'angels'; pornographic images of women are on display in newsagents, in newspapers, in advertising. Women are expected to remain silent about their unhappiness with their lot – if they complain they are described as over-emotional, hysterical, whining. Women receive little support in their efforts to fight back. If male probation officers are not prepared to take these issues seriously, cede some privilege and listen to women, they will not be able to work progressively with male offenders.

## Women in relation to male clients

It is normal in this society for a woman to be defined according to her relationship with a man, rather than as a person in her own right. Simone de Beauvoir (1974, p.16) wrote 'This humanity is male and man defines woman not in herself but as relative to him. . .' The final section will consider the roles and stereotypes attached to the women associated with male clients in probation practice, and consider some alternative approaches.

*Women as community carers*   Feminist commentators have pointed out the (unpaid and unacknowledged) work that women carry out in the community providing care for children, the elderly, the sick, the mentally ill. Women bear the brunt of community-care policies and the consequences of public expenditure cuts that have such a neat congruence with these policies (Wilson, 1977; Barrett and McIntosh, 1982). In probation different, but parallel, demands are made on women; for instance the wives and girlfriends of men in prison are expected to keep home and family together in order to help the men settle down to a stable and crime-free life on release. The difficulties of these women have not gone undocumented, but probation practice has done little to produce improvements in their lot. Rather probation officers encourage them to struggle on: 'Our professional concern for the prisoner leads to a desire to preserve the status quo and deters a "rock of the boat" by acknowledging the conflicts inherent in the woman's position' (Wilkinson, Cherry and Williams, 1981, p.2). A traditional approach to such women has been the setting up of prisoners' wives groups. However their function has not been straightforward help but assistance aimed at making the process of the prisoner's resettlement easier for the family (NACRO, 1978b).

*Women as pacifiers and civilisers* Another role attributed to women is that of home-maker; the provider of a 'free area' of pleasure and satisfaction to offset the aridity of 'work' (Wilson, 1980). Women are expected to work at making the home a pleasant place where men can be rewarded for being the wage-earner, be cossetted, soothed and civilised. In probation work there is an assumption that if a wife or girlfriend can properly provide all that a home should offer, her man will be deterred from criminal associations and activity and will not need to seek refuge in the pub with his delinquent peer group. The love and devotion of a good woman is thought to be worth any amount of work by a probation officer. This hopeful belief often forms the basis of lenient recommendations in social enquiry reports. The *South London Press* (14 March 1980) reported: 'Although a man had a 'terrible' record with convictions spreading over four pages, he was put on probation, provided he attended a day training centre, the judge saying there was every indication that since marrying he would lead a different life.'

*Women as responsible for male crime* An alternative assumption made is that if women do not behave 'appropriately' they are responsible for causing male crime. Carol Smart (1976, p.178) wrote: 'Women are the ones who are believed to cause their men to act, usually through manipulation. . . Mothers are held to be responsible for the delinquency of their children.' Examples of this abound in social enquiry reports:

> Mrs X has made a genuine attempt to be what she considers 'a good mother'. However in her attempt to be this she has overwhelmed her son, who has been totally stifled in her presence. It appears that one of the few ways by which Mr X can prove his independence is his involvement in criminal activity.

Another stereotype is the avaricious wife, illustrated by Geoffrey (Tailgunner) Parkinson's (1983) cameo of 'Pretty Polly': 'So now she just lolls around in her dressing gown at midday, half-nagging her unemployed husband to bring in a little extra money either by getting a job – or "doing" one.' Common targets for blame in writing on sexual offenders are 'frigid wives' and 'dominating mothers'. However, such labels may simply refer to behaviour that challenges conventional expectations of feminine behaviour – submissive, dependent and nurturant. It is surely questionable for probation officers to use such value judgements as operational concepts in their practice.

The theme of 'blaming women' also emerges in some descriptions of family therapy, especially since a key concept in the method is 'appropriate role'. A task of family therapy is to 'identify and talk about family myths: for example, that Dad is bad and drinks all the money when in reality it is Mother who is a bad housekeeper' (Ireland and Dawes, 1975, p.115). Women are often blamed for crimes where they are the victim, and held responsible whatever their behaviour; 'being too talkative or too quiet, too sexual or not sexual enough, too often pregnant, or not frequently enough, all seemed to be provocations' (Dobash and Dobash, 1979, p.135).

*Points for practice*

Again it is important for probation officers to examine the assumptions they are making about women in their work and to *carry any conclusions into practice*. They must consider whether they are unjustifiably attributing blame to women; expecting women to adopt subordinate, demeaning or inappropriate roles, assuming that women will shoulder domestic burdens or can be responsible for their husbands' behaviour. It must be recognised that women are people in their own right with needs, desires, views and expectations and not simply other peoples' wives, girlfriends and mothers (Corrigan and Leonard, 1978). Every area of practice should be influenced by this reappraisal. In social enquiry reports, probation officers should be *careful of using arguments* about the good influence of a wife or girlfriend. Again it can be argued that such a tactical ploy is acceptable. A possible way forward is to discuss it with the woman concerned; explain your reasons for wanting to use the tactic, and the advantages and disadvantages before making a final decision.

In general probation officers should be aiming to *encourage wider choices for women.* This means not making assumptions about the female role, finding out about the expanded training and educational opportunities now becoming available for women and actively supporting those who want to take advantage of this. Such action will include finding out about child-care facilities, or arguing for them so that women are able to take up new opportunities. In dealing with prisoners' wives, probation officers should endeavour to *take a more even-handed approach,* recognising a potential conflict of interest between partners. There cannot be absolute prescriptions for practice here, and difficulties will be dealt with in different ways according to the family. However, probation officers should assist a woman whose partner is in custody both practically and emotionally in such a way as to allow her to make real choices about the future of that relationship. If probation officers feel that the conflict of interests is too great, they should put such women in contact with another helping agency or colleague. Improved accommodation for men released from custody – a legitimate demand in its own right – might reduce the pressure on mothers, wives and girlfriends who are reluctant to have them back on release. This even-handed approach is also important in family work, especially with the parents of juvenile offenders. This means actively bringing fathers into discussions about family matters, thus reinforcing the view that they too bear responsibility for the care and upbringing of children.

### In conclusion

This chapter has attempted to point to some areas where fundamental issues about the role and status of women need attention in progressive probation practice. It has indicated some ways in which probation officers could examine their practice and move towards change. A constant theme has been the need for probation officers to reassess and re-evaluate their thinking. This must be done rigorously if progress is to be made, as Dale Spender's research on women's contributions to discussions illustrates. She tape-recorded mixed-sex discussions in which she took part and evaluated what she thought had taken place against the taped evidence. She found:

> While I *believed* that I did not give more attention to men than women in mixed-sex talk, that I did not turn to them for guidance, defer to their opinions, seek confirmation from them, or favour them at the expense of women, the tapes told a different story. (Spender, 1980, p.135)

If such an error can be made by a committed feminist who is consciously trying to act in an egalitarian and non-sexist way, we should all re-examine our own behaviour.

# 6

# Probation, Working for Social Change?

Bill Beaumont

'Every social worker is almost certain to be also an agitator.' (Attlee, 1920)

Working for social change has long featured as one element in discussions of social work but Clement Attlee's bold assertion over-estimates the commitment made to it in social work practice. Kathleen Woodroofe identifies social casework and social reform as competing and divergent strands in the early development of social work, but is in no doubt which approach dominated:

> The social worker saw herself primarily as a technician whose first responsibility was to her client, rather than as a crusader bent on curing the maladies of society – social work has always had a distinct distaste for any action which threatened to distrurb the *status quo*. (Woodroofe, 1962, p.203)

The tension between the two approaches arises from the dominant view that problems stem mainly from individual weaknesses which will respond only to personal attention. Thus even where the need for reform is accepted, and supported, its importance is diminished. There is some evidence (Woodroofe, 1962; Lees, 1972) that reform ideas were more influential in social work during the depression of the 1930s but they were firmly relegated to the background by the strong dominance of psychotherapeutic ideas in post-war social work. The reform orientation has continued to be the poor relation of social work theory and practice.

The 're-discovery' of poverty in the 1960s, growing disillu-

sion with psychodynamic casework and the emergence of a
radical critique of social work have combined to encourage a
cautious re-emergence of social change as a goal in social
work. The systems or unitary approach envisaged a more
diverse role for the social worker – the ubiquitous 'change
agent' could 'target' a social work agency, the community or
even policy issues (Pincus and Minahan, 1973; Goldstein,
1973). Drawing on that approach, the British Association of
Social Workers identified 'agent of social change' as one of 20
social work roles and in their 'Code of Ethics for Social Work'
placed a positive duty on social workers 'to bring to the
attention of those in power, and of the general public, ways in
which the activities of government, society or agencies, create
or contribute to hardship or militate against their relief'
(BASW, 1977, p.68). This position was endorsed in the
government sponsored Barclay Report (1982).

Social reform has been more marginal in the development
of probation work, which has traditionally been preoccupied
with the reclamation of the individual offender. However the
last 15 years have seen social change belatedly emerge as
a legitimate concern in probation work. Joan King (1969)
tentatively suggested that probation officers should actively
point out gaps and anomalies in social provision and agitate
for improvement. David Haxby (1978, p.194) argues more
directly that 'social workers, including probation officers,
have their part to play in the development of pressure for
political change. . .'. The National Association of Probation
Officers has as one of its objectives 'To formulate and execute
policies to improve . . . the criminal justice system and the
social welfare of the community' (NAPO, 1980).

Despite these recent developments, most of the comment
about working for social change within social work has remained at the level of abstract theory or declamatory support.
There has been a lack of definition about what may be
possible, how to approach such work and how it can be
incorporated in social work practice. The systems approach
provided little practice guidance for 'the agent of social
change' and has been criticised for avoiding important ethical
questions and contentious policy issues (McLeod and
Dominelli, 1982). Over the last decade many more probation

officers have become critical of the social injustices we see in our work and therefore more sympathetic to the idea of pressing for change. Collectively, through NAPO, probation officers have been prepared to be allied with campaigns for criminal justice and social policy reforms. However, in every-day probation practice a campaigning approach has remained exceptional, and anger about the experiences of clients is still largely dissipated rather than turned into pressure for social change.

In *Probation Work* we identified 'campaigning action' as an important feature of a socialist approach to probation prac-tice (Walker and Beaumont, 1981). In this chapter I aim to examine more fully the ways in which such work can be developed and incorporated in probation practice. By 'cam-paigning work' I mean work by probation officers which draws upon their experience of social problems and injus-tices, gained through contact with clients, and uses that information in pursuit of relevant social change. There is therefore a close connection between campaigning work and other aspects of probation practice. It does not involve aban-doning immediate assistance to clients, but complements such help with action aimed at tackling the causes of shared social problems. It forms an integral part of an honest and princi-pled response to the difficulties experienced by clients. As well as seeking immediate reforms and opposing regressive developments, campaigning work can expose the workings of the criminal justice and social systems to critical debate. As probation officers, we must find time and use opportunities to take our knowledge and experience beyond individual proba-tion practice and into a real, widespread and consistent engagement in campaigning work.

## Campaigning work – case studies

Three recent examples of campaigning which involved proba-tion officers should help to illustrate the opportunities which arise in probation work. Between them they involve a range of issues about content, aims, methods and tactics, but are by no means exhaustive of the possibilities for such work. These examples provide the basis for the discussion of the potential for, and limitations of, campaigning work which follows.

## Operation Major

This unprecedented joint police/DHSS swoop used a dummy benefits office in Oxford for the mass arrest of 283 claimants suspected of fraud. It was acclaimed by the media whose lead stories talked wildly of a £1 500 000 swindle, involving organised bands of travelling fraudsters, master-minded by a 'Mr Big'. This was a sensational 'scrounger' story with enormous impact and provided a major boost for the government's campaign to squeeze benefits. *Poor Law* (Franey, 1983) provides a detailed, critical examination of Operation Major; here I will concentrate on the reaction from probation officers. Although the police had forewarned local courts and prisons (and press!), the probation service had not been told of special court sittings. On learning, they arranged emergency cover for the courts which sat till 11.00 pm. Probation officers and solicitors were denied normal access to defendants waiting to appear. Efforts to offer bail hostel places were brushed aside as the courts remanded 152 out of 175 defendants in custody. Arrangements were then made for each person to be interviewed by prison probation officers and a network of bail hostel places was available when they reappeared. Over half the defendants were known to the service, mostly through attendance at a voluntary probation day centre for homeless people. Nevertheless reports were requested in only six cases, as the courts imprisoned almost all those who admitted offences. Despite organising to provide positive assistance to defendants and the courts, the probation service was not allowed to play its normal role.

Realising the wider significance of these extraordinary events, probation officers recognised early on the need to respond at a different level to the injustices and misleading coverage of Operation Major. They found their concern shared by some solicitors and the local claimants' union, who formed a defence committee. They helped monitor court hearings to provide hard information to counter press re-

ports. They secured the backing of NAPO locally and nationally. In the next week NAPO and CHAR added to early
criticisms by publishing strong attacks on the operation. They
questioned the need for the swoop, publicised the denial of
legal rights and attitude of the courts and highlighted the
inadequate benefits and housing provision available to homeless persons. This criticism got some publicity and the BBC
minority programme Grapevine (12 October 1982) confronted a government minister with some of the critics.
CHAR played a central role in compiling and publishing a
report, *Poor Law*, together with four other organisations –
Claimants' Defence Committee, CPAG, NAPO and NCCL.
It received extensive publicity, produced a parliamentary
debate and meetings with ministers from the DHSS and
Home Office. It was discussed in the Thames Valley police
committee and the local council. Oxford probation officers
aired their criticisms directly in a special meeting with magistrates.

The involvement of probation officers in this campaign
arose directly from their daily work in the courts. They
combined good probation practice (rendered ineffective by
the attitude of the courts) with campaigning work on the
wider issues. They were able to work co-operatively with
other groups and learn from their greater experience. Working through the union provided financial support and some
protection, although they also found a relatively sympathetic
response from management. The impact of this reactive
campaign was considerable. It provided some counter to the
effect of the original 'scrounger' story, exposed the arbitrary
nature of the operation and led to critical debate on both
benefit levels and the government's aggressive stance on
benefit fraud. There is evidence to suggest it persuaded the
DHSS to abandon large-scale swoops. Although smaller-
scale exercises have continued, the police and the courts have
behaved less arbitrarily. It led directly to an increase in
benefit paid to homeless claimants (by about £6 per week
from November 1983), reversing an earlier cut. Locally the
campaign made a substantial impact on the council's housing
policy (CHAR, 1983).

## PROS

The work and development of PROS (Programme for the Reform of the Laws on Soliciting) has been well documented by Eileen McLeod (1981; 1982), a founder member. As a probation officer in Birmingham she helped establish a drop-in centre, with an advice and welfare function, to extend contact with women involved in soliciting. Discussions with women using the centre focused attention on issues of law reform and in 1976 the campaigning group PROS was founded. Its aims were to end imprisonment for soliciting, abolish legal use of the term 'common prostitute' and ultimately decriminalise soliciting (McLeod, 1981). Although attracting a range of other supporters (including probation officers and social workers) the campaign has built its activity mainly on the direct participation of women who have been prostitutes. The self-help focus has been carefully protected by ensuring that prostitutes speak for themselves in the group's representations.

The campaign established groups in several other cities and provides loose co-ordination. It has had to resist pressures to adopt a welfare orientation in order to concentrate upon its main aim of legal reform. An important source of support has been the women's movement. PROS adopted a conventional pressure group approach in its efforts to influence public opinion and secure legislative change. Together with the English Collective of Prostitutes, it has succeeded in establishing a public voice for prostitutes. It has received considerable media attention and, despite the attendant difficulties (McLeod, 1982), has used these opportunities to press the case for reform. PROS has also given evidence to recent official enquiries which had never previously heard from prostitutes' representatives. This organising work helped to uncover, and then add to, considerable public sympathy with the case for reform. Parliamentary lobbying by ECP and PROS produced private members' initiatives in 1979 and 1981 which attracted growing support. Early pessimism amongst MPs gave way to increasing optimism (McLeod, 1982) and an amendment to the Criminal Justice Act 1982 ended imprisonment as a direct penalty for the offence of soliciting.

This is an example of a probation officer's involvement in a campaign growing directly out of her work with clients. It led to an organisation in which the 'client' group played a leading role. Initial probation service support for an advice/welfare focus did not extend to the campaigning development, and direct links between the service and PROS were quickly severed. However, probation officers have continued to support the work of the group and NAPO affiliated to the campaign in 1978. PROS has achieved the legal change which was its first objective, although prostitutes have continued to be imprisoned for failing to pay fines. Magistrates in London have vociferously criticised their own 'lack of powers' and this limited reform will have to be defended against these attacks.

## The curfew

During a Commons committee debate on the Criminal Justice Act 1982 a Conservative backbencher, prompted by the Magistrates' Association, proposed the imposition of a curfew as a new penalty, for offenders aged under 21, to be enforced by the police. NAPO, already monitoring the bill's progress, responded quickly with a briefing paper to committee members (20 March 1982) arguing that it would place parents in an invidious position, worsen family relationships, prove difficult to enforce, damage relations between police and young people and be ineffective in preventing offences. Labour MPs, hesitant at first (on the argument that anything is better than custody), were persuaded to oppose the curfew vigorously in committee. The government however agreed to give it further consideration; less firm opposition from other social work organisations encouraged them to think of a modified curfew as a condition of supervision for juveniles. NAPO successfully lobbied for stronger resistance from interested organisations such as BASW, NACRO, NCCL and NYB. Despite growing opposition the government pressed ahead to introduce the 'night restriction order' as a condition of supervision by 79 votes to 64 in the House of Lords.

Its Annual General Meeting in October 1982 committed NAPO to continued opposition, calling on members 'to refuse to recommend, supervise or co-operate with orders' containing either night restriction orders or negative condi-

tions (conditions prohibiting specified activities). Such conditions were seen as unacceptably shifting the probation officer's role towards routine surveillance. NAPO was thus committed to resist these conditions through industrial action.
Support was sought from social workers through BASW and
NALGO; both advised members not to recommend such
conditions, but stopped short of industrial action. NAPO's
strong stance produced a conciliatory response from both the
Home Office and probation managers, anxious to head off a
conflict with the courts. The 'night restriction order' became
available to the courts in May 1983 but all the indications at
the time of writing are that very few curfews have been
imposed.

This defensive campaign succeeded in uniting probation
officers against an oppressive new measure in the criminal
justice system and spreading that opposition amongst other
social workers, pressure groups and even some probation
managers. It differs from the previous examples in being a
campaign initiated and conducted by the union. That the
campaign failed to dissuade a determined government from
legislating highlights the weak position of NAPO relative to
the Magistrates' Association. The lack of wider public support on criminal justice issues produced a narrowly based
campaign. Its location in the union structure was crucial when
industrial action became the only way to continue opposition.
The use of direct action appears so far to have prevented any
significant use of the curfew, but so long as it is a potential
condition the possibility of a difficult confrontation remains.
One feature of this campaign was that opposition to the new
proposal was weakened by the existence of precursors which
had not been opposed – curfews as conditions of bail and rules
imposed on probation hostel residents.

## Campaigning work – potential and limitations

A fundamental criticism of social casework is its failure to
tackle economic and social problems faced by clients. Campaigning work offers one way of overcoming that limitation.
It may produce reforms which make a more significant,

widespread and long-term contribution to the welfare of the client group than individual assistance ever could. Thus for PROS, 'if the removal of imprisonment were brought about, it would at a stroke remove the need for hundreds of mopping up operations . . .' (McLeod, 1982, p.124). There is considerable potential for campaigning work to become an integral part of probation work, routinely drawing upon the experience of practice to press for relevant change.

Probation officers have often, explicitly or implicitly, supported the view that reforms were irrelevant because real problems lay in individual maladjustment. Active support from within state welfare agencies makes an important contribution to pressures for change. This is particularly important within the criminal justice system: 'It matters that there are probation officers prepared to state publicly that prison is destructive, that there are unjust laws, that law enforcement is discriminatory . . . The whole burden of opposition and exposure otherwise falls on those processed by the system, offenders whose credibility is easily undermined' (Walker and Beaumont, 1981, p.169).

The examples give some indication of the wide range of experience and information which probation officers accumulate on *social policy issues* such as inadequate benefit levels, homelessness, treatment of social security fraud, lack of opportunity for women; and *criminal justice issues* such as bail refusal, inappropriate use of custody, unjust laws, complaints about police practices and oppressive 'law and order' developments. In these areas and many more – including the effects of poverty, poor housing and racial discrimination, the prosecution of trivial offences, excessive fines and the destructiveness of imprisonment – probation officers have knowledge which could be used constructively in campaigning work.

Our contribution can be at various levels. In some fields we can provide information and case examples to established, well-organised campaigns like CPAG, CHAR, LAG and NCCL. Personal involvement in such campaigns will help us learn and improve relevant skills, which can be imported back into our probation work. Smaller, more local campaigns could benefit from the skills and facilities which probation officers can offer. Eileen McLeod spells out the significance of such assistance in the early development of PROS: 'As a campaign it could not have got anywhere without free access to the following – photocopying, secretarial services, paper, postage, printing, telephones, transport, and on average four days' labour per week incorporating a wide range of professional talents and knowledge' (McLeod, 1982, p.132).

On some issues the union will provide an appropriate vehicle for campaigning work. NAPO branches have criticised sentencing practices in local courts, providing some protection for the officers who have supplied information. Nationally, NAPO has only recently started to encourage and use information from members in campaigning but there is clearly considerable potential in this development. Already it has enabled NAPO to play a leading part in exposing the use of police cells for remand prisoners, and in pressing for a 110-day limit on custodial remands. Even without a high level of practical involvement, probation officers' support for a campaign can help to increase its credibility and influence. NAPO's affiliation to PROS 'enhanced the campaign's public standing, besides providing support and cover for probation officers around the country who want to organise in connection with it' (McLeod, 1981, p.73).

The goals set in campaigning will also be at different levels. Some campaigns will be for limited reforms achievable in some form within a reasonable period. PROS secured its first objective in six years, although as already noted even small reforms need to be vigorously defended. The Conservative 'new right' have produced attacks on long-established reforms; the repeated attempts to re-introduce hanging, 1979–83, are a striking example. Inevitably in this political climate even limited reforms take second place to defensive campaigns preoccupied with protecting existing welfare provision and resisting oppressive developments. Setting goals for such campaigns needs particular care. This government has often succeeded in drawing criticism to exaggerated elements in its proposals, allowing a 'compromise' which leaves the main proposal intact. Thus when compulsion and a £10 cut in allowance were dropped from the original YTS proposal, many critics were left supporting a scheme which paid a standstill allowance and included coercion through benefits' reduction. Essentially defensive campaigns can sometimes produce small reforms; Operation Major, for instance, led to an increase in benefit for homeless claimants. They may also lay the ground for progressive developments when the political climate is changed. Other campaigns deliberately make ambitious demands which are unlikely to be realised rapidly. It is important in a time of political and social regression, that sight is not lost of progressive aims. These campaigns can play an important ideological role in exposing injustices and promoting critical debate.

Campaigning organisations face difficult issues in setting demands. Thomas Mathieson (1974) warns of the opposing dangers of incorporation and exclusion. In the search for relevance and credibility it is easy to adopt goals which represent little change, thus posing no real alternative and becoming *incorporated*. More radical demands may pose an alternative but lead to the campaigner being defined out of the argument and thus *excluded*. The aim must be to avoid both dangers, to achieve the 'competing contradiction' (Mathieson, 1974, p.14). Campaigns face acute dilemmas in assessing the value of short-term gains as opposed to continued pressure for more far-reaching change. PROS, for instance, has been criticised from a feminist viewpoint for its failure to pursue general improvements for women which might encourage them to leave prostitution (McLeod and Dominelli, 1982). At worst some reforms serve to support and legitimise existing social arrangements and obstruct more fundamental change. Socialists need to analyse carefully which demands will in this way prove to be reformist rather than genuinely progressive. It is arguable that the recent parliamentary decisions to end imprisonment for soliciting and vagrancy could prove reformist, weakening efforts to decriminalise these offences.

These difficulties are heightened for socialists by the contradictory nature of reform within the capitalist system. Reforms can bring real benefits for working-class people but also strengthen and legitimate the existing exploitative social order. Thus, during the recession, unemployment benefit has been a vital resource for many but helped to defuse unemployment as a political issue. Reforms will be mediated in the interests of capital, affecting both the form and delivery of provision. Often reform will be partial – strong support from the black community produced success for the 'Scrap Sus' campaign, 'but the Criminal Attempts Act 1981, which repealed sus, also created *new* criminal offences of interfering with a motor vehicle and attempt' (Gordon, 1983, p.33). In practice probation officers are likely to be involved with a range of demands of differing levels of significance. A critical awareness of their relative importance and prospects of success is required. Realism about our relative contribution will allow a measured view to be taken when achievements are evaluated. Small gains will not be regarded as a sufficient end in themselves, but neither will they be dismissed as irrelevant, thus adding to frustration and despair.

Arguments and methods used in campaigning are also problematic. Superficially attractive and useful arguments can prove counter-productive. The use made of prison overcrowding by penal reform groups helped generate public concern, but was readily co-opted by the Conservatives to justify extensive prison building. The case studies illustrate a range of campaigning methods – the preparation of publicity material, use of the media, securing allies, direct parliamentary work, contact with government departments and industrial action. Each campaign used a mix of approaches and such eclecticism is likely to feature in most campaigning work. Each method poses its own problems and limitations which need to be tackled in practice. For instance, direct publicity material reaches a limited audience and usually it will be important to reach a wider public by using the media. This is fraught with difficulties, including the media's control over the terms and content of coverage. While important to recognise that the media does represent a powerful set of vested interests, it is possible to make and take opportunities for helpful exposure. Parliamentary work has clear limitations, which are heightened at a time when the government has a huge majority. However failure to argue the case for change concedes defeat by default. Many changes will depend upon legislative measures and so campaigns will often need to include parliamentary work in their plans. This is not the place for a discussion of the relative merits of parliamentary and extra-parliamentary action – most campaigns need to combine the two approaches. In much campaigning work probation officers will necessarily be restricted to using methods of argument and persuasion. The campaign against the curfew, however, shows that on some issues and at some times industrial action, or other direct action, will be a possible approach. Effective direct or industrial action is not easy to organise, but can shift the balance of power which is often a more important barrier to reform than any lack of evidence or logical argument. Such action, especially that which can be portrayed as unlawful, can lead to increased risk and decreased support and therefore requires careful consideration.

The pursuit of social change is inevitably political, and campaigning work by probation officers, even if modest in its goals, is likely to be controversial in practice. Probation officers can expect some pressure, arising from their position as state employees, to keep campaigning work outside working hours or even to curtail their 'out of hours' activities. For instance, probation officers have been excluded from prisons because of support for PROP, excluded from court by magistrates offended by criticism of sentencing practices, asked to curtail active membership of CHE and discriminated against in employment over trade-union activism. An officer convicted of an offence arising from political protest could face disciplinary action. There are limits to the campaigning which can be done through employment as a probation officer. These are likely to become more restrictive as the state becomes more coercive, as indicated by recent dramatic curtailment of the political rights of civil servants. Despite these potential limitations, the boundaries of probation work are still sufficiently diffuse and broad for a substantial range of campaigning work to form a legitimate activity within the probation officer's role. Even where some involvement has to be outside that role, probation officers have flexible working arrangements which can facilitate practical involvement in campaigns. Although the limitations are real, there is considerable scope for increased engagement in campaigning work within these boundaries. A widespread development of this work by probation officers will both test out and stretch the limits of the politically possible.

## A campaigning approach in probation practice

This final section considers some practice issues encountered in differing levels of involvement in campaigning.

### Using practice experience

The first requirement is alertness to the significance of our experience and how it relates to policy issues. Probation officers undervalue both the importance of their knowledge and its potential impact. We can provide campaigns with a flow of useful, raw case material. Occasionally a case is such a clear example of abuse that it alone proves a powerful vehicle in pressing for reform. The Confait case, for instance, led to an enquiry into police interrogation methods. Similarly a case may be sufficiently dramatic to be used as a news story. More often, we can contribute examples of everyday injustices for use in compiling a dossier of evidence.

Having identified potentially useful information, you then need to work out its best use. This may simply involve locating a campaign with an existing mechanism for using case material. Organisations like NCCL, LAG and Justice receive a flow of legal casework which is sifted for strong cases; the Erroll Madden case became a leading example of police abuse of stop and search. It may involve contacting campaigns to see if they can use your example; even if not already collecting material they may be interested, particularly if you can promise a flow of information. The union, locally or nationally, may be prepared to collate material and encourage other members to look for similar evidence. Where a local problem is identified, you may be able to interest your team or a local agency. A particular case may have several uses. The wide range of issues encountered in probation practice can create a problem in identifying issues, collecting information and gauging its usefulness. This can be countered by pooling information amongst the team, the probation area and through the union. Campaigning work will be assisted by, and in turn may encourage, more collective approaches to probation work.

Participation in campaigning at this level requires only a modest commitment of time and effort. In the first instance, a brief note of case examples will usually suffice. You can retain more detailed information, and be prepared to contact the individual concerned again, should further details be required. Follow-up work may be involved if the case proves to be a particularly strong example. Where a case is used in a dossier it will be possible to guarantee anonymity, but securing consent even to such use is good practice. Where a case leads to a news story or legal case-work then the client will be subject to some public exposure. Caution is then necessary and participation should be on the basis of informed consent, once potential difficulties have been properly explored. Despite the immediate pressures of work with clients you will find it worthwhile if you make time to use practice experience in this way. It helps combat the frustration of endlessly patching up problems that could be prevented, and it is satisfying to see material you have provided helping to make the case for change.

## Developing campaigning work

For some people, and on some issues, a closer involvement in direct campaigning will be appropriate. They will need to learn and develop new skills in preparing and presenting material, in seeking and securing support. Working with existing campaigns, and in the union, can help develop skills through observation and personal participation. It will also increase awareness of the potential for campaigning work and provide ideas on how to take it forward. Before a new campaigning effort is launched some research is necessary to ensure that opportunities to learn from, and co-operate with, existing campaigns are not missed.

A common requirement in campaigning is the preparation of publicity material – leaflets, pamphlets, articles and/or reports. These demand the development of writing skills so that material is concise, readable, descriptive and jargon-free. Complex issues and experiences need considerable simplification so a clear and understandable message emerges. Thought needs to be given to the intended audience – different approaches may be needed to appeal to interested professionals, the general public, MPs or government departments. Good design and attractive presentation also make a real difference to effectiveness. Public speaking skills also need development. Practice and good preparation will help anyone present arguments more effectively; sincerity is often more convincing than natural eloquence. Again the emphasis needs to be on direct, clear and jargon-free speech.

Most campaigns actively seek media coverage; all need to respond to press interest and defend against bad publicity. This can be difficult, but experience suggests it is a necessary struggle and that it is possible to secure constructive coverage on a wide range of issues. A few basic lessons in use of the media can enable the beginner to start building experience. These include how to gain access, how to write a good press release, using the Press Association to respond quickly to developments, what to expect in interview and opportunities to practice all these elements. NAPO now provides basic training for branch officials. Denis McShane (1979) has written a very useful handbook for trade unionists and community activists. It is easier to secure coverage in prestige dailies (the *Guardian* and *The Times*), the specialist press and on minority broadcasts than in the truly mass media outlets. Peak-time television, popular radio and the tabloid press are difficult to penetrate and most likely to distort through compression. Local papers and, in particular, local radio are eager for ready-made news and easy to use; the inexperience of, and pressures on, their reporters enable you to get your message over with a minimum of 'media bias'! Often reporters will want to interview people with first-hand experience. Care is necessary in exposing clients to such contacts, particularly if identification will leave them vulnerable (see McLeod, 1982, for problems caused for some PROS members).

In campaigning work, probation officers need to seek support and this involves making wider contacts than is usual in the job. We will need to contact local authority and government departments, MPs, councillors, campaigns, trade unions, tenants' associations and other community groups. Seeking out and making links is an important stage in campaign development. Alliances around limited aims are possible between quite disparate groups but caution is needed in avoiding allies who seek to limit goals, differ significantly on methods or arguments, or desert when the going gets tough. Effective lobbying in councils and parliament requires some detailed knowledge and considerable effort. With care good use can be made of local councillors and MPs, special interest parliamentary groupings and parliamentary debates, all of which can make news as well as contribute to administrative and legislative change.

## Local use of campaigning

The same skills can be used to tackle problems at local level. Ted Perry and Dave Burnham (1977) described a campaign they launched as probation officers in Mansfield to change local authority policy towards homeless persons. On the same issue, Steve McGrath (1983) has urged probation officers to campaign locally using guidelines from CHAR. The West Midlands Probation Service (1981) monitored contact with black offenders and made proposals to counteract racial discrimination. To these examples can be added many more possibilities. A service's own policies may be unhelpful, for instance, over use of the befriending fund or community service provision for women. The collection of evidence and application of concerted pressure may produce improvements. Colleagues may be suggesting custody in court reports or failing to recommend alternatives – monitoring of reports and results may encourage changed practices. A team could monitor sentencing at local courts; magistrates may be surprised by the cumulative effect of their decisions, embarassed by particular cases or the severity of some individuals, or convinced that they use custody more than they should. They may be persuaded to change specific practices or their general approach, and if unconvinced by facts may respond to public criticism. Where a local DHSS office causes particular difficulties, isolated complaints can be turned into a case for improvement and taken up with the manager, local civil service trade unions, regional office or if necessary the local MP and councillors.

Local use of a campaigning approach does not depend upon, but may have some overlap with, the development of community work approaches in probation practice. Although some teams and projects have sought to broaden their focus from work with individual offenders, experimentation with community involvement by probation officers has remained limited. A widespread commitment by the probation service to the aim of crime reduction through 'micro-structural environmental improvement' has been advocated (Bottoms and McWilliams, 1979) and has now been endorsed by the Home Office (1984). There is potential for progressive developments in probation practice through increased community involvement, although lessons must be learnt from the wider field of community work and particular problems arise if such work is tied to a narrow crime prevention goal.

The potential use of campaigning work in probation practice is only now starting to be explored. In this chapter I have argued that it is an important contribution to a progressive practice which can overcome some of the limitations of individual case work. Campaigning work can, and should, become an integral part of probation work; as probation officers we can, and should, more systematically take our knowledge and experience beyond individual practice. By doing so we can help to promote progressive social change and make a more profound contribution to the welfare of our clients.

# 7

# Groupwork with Offenders

Paul Senior

Groupwork, whilst much talked about, has until recently not had a massive impact in actual probation practice. The dominance of an individualised approach at all levels has possibly contributed to a reluctance to widen the scope of work with offenders. Probation officers themselves have not universally embraced teamwork approaches which at their best can emphasise sharing and collaborative work. If they are unwilling to genuinely develop their work in a group-oriented manner, this will in turn inhibit the commitment to and credence for work with groups of offenders. This chapter will look at groupwork developments in the context of a socialist approach to probation work, and discuss the possibilities for the development of positive potential in groupwork from that perspective. The limitations of groupwork for the socialist will emerge from this analysis, which will include consideration of the legal context and the appropriateness of conditional attendance. I will conclude by looking at the links to be made between the personal situation and the political and economic position of the offender, an essential but difficult task for the socialist.

## Developments and assumptions

Parsloe (1972) observed that whilst there was an increasing investment in groupwork training there was still relatively little groupwork taking place. In many ways that picture would still hold true today, although there have been a number of stimuli towards the development of groupwork with offenders in the past 15 years. The assumption of after-care responsibilities has led to the exploration of more pertinent ways of offering social work help and advice to prisoners and their families. These typically include social skills groups, pre-release groups and forms of group therapy at more specialist prisons such as Grendon. Often these groups are shared with, and even developed by, prison staff themselves. In the community, support groups for the wives and families of prisoners have been a constant feature in most probation areas. Another development in the 1970s, following changes in legislation, has been the mushrooming of intermediate treatment, particularly towards the latter half of the decade. Often intermediate treatment has been seen as synonymous with groupwork. Although there would appear to be some continuity with the adventure training of earlier decades this work has focused more directly on offenders and their needs, rather than on probation officers' preferences. The development of day training centres provided an opportunity for probation officers to try out groupwork methods. In their early days they experimented with the more esoteric groupwork methods taken largely from the field of social psychology, without notable success however. Such therapeutic approaches, making use of an array of techniques and philosophies such as gestalt therapy, transactional analysis and T-groups, have had their individual proponents within the service, but little generalised impact. More recently, day training centres have provided a showcase for the development of social skills training and methods. Social skills, a generic description for a range of remedial help to individuals or groups, has been taken up more generally and used in voluntary day centres, probation hostels, induction groups, intermediate treatment and prisoners' groups amongst others.

Haxby (1978, p.230) comments that the limited use of groupwork is a result of its somewhat nebulous place in probation work 'at present it is seen largely as an "optional extra" for some clients'. Certainly explicit management commitment to groupwork has been hard to obtain. Much groupwork has been the result of individual initiative and has only been sustained through working extra hours and stretching personal resources. Thus whilst working with groups has undoubtedly grown, its forms are still often idiosyncratic and rarely systematic, although increased use of social skills techniques has become more widespread in both groupwork and individual work.

Socialists must be able to look critically at existing practice, evaluate underlying assumptions and, where necessary challenge the basis upon which certain groups operate, before developing an alternative socialist strategy. Three examples of questionable assumptions illustrate this point. Firstly as Collins and Behan (1981, p.89) write, intermediate treatment is 'Redolent of pastoral assumptions about the merits of an outdoor life, the view that an offender has only to be put deep into the country for him to mop up virtue by some obscure process of moral osmosis as he labours up to his ankles in manure.' Activity-based groups clearly do work best when the leaders have an interest in, and enthusiasm for, the particular activity, and certainly excursions to the countryside have been enjoyed by offenders under my supervision. What must be avoided is the crude ideas about socialisation implicit in some such programmes. Crucially they ignore the wider social context of offending. Secondly prisoners' wives groups raise the issue of inappropriate labelling. While such groups are often supportive they may divert attention away from the women's needs by focusing on aspects of their traditional role which they may wish to face and question during this enforced separation. Too often *we* decide what the needs of our clients are. We should not assume that distress and difficulty arise simply because of the loss of the male; many of the identified problems were probably previously present. Labelling such groups as 'prisoners' wives groups may crucially determine how, and for whom, they operate.

The third illustration links with a predominant socialist concern in all social work – the emphasis on changing the behaviour of the individual as the target of casework, and treatment models of either a psychoanalytic or behaviourist type. Assumptions which appear to underpin much groupwork do not escape the problems associated with individual casework. Indeed Rothman and Papell (1977) classify three main groupwork orientations and identify the remedial model as one predominant mode; it is 'Clearly a clinical model focused upon helping the malperforming individual to achieve a more desirable state of social functioning ... The group is viewed as a tool or context for treatment of the individual. Diagnostic goals for each individual as established by the worker supersede group goals' (p.141). A socialist analysis, using a framework for understanding which asserts the necessity for a wider structural perspective, must be wary of simply treating the group as another medium for individual behaviour change. Discussion about intermediate treatment in recent years has often contained the rhetoric of correctionalist assumptions. We should seek to challenge the attention paid to personal inadequacy and pathology in groupwork so as not to repeat the errors of individual work.

## The legal context

As probation officers we have to recognise that we work largely within the criminal justice system and what this means for the aims, tasks and nature of the groupwork we undertake. Understanding the legal context is therefore important, since it determines and circumscribes the groupwork which can develop. There has recently been a growth in the use of extra conditions in probation and supervision orders. Discussion within the probation service on this issue has been bedevilled by a crude polarisation between advocates of voluntary attendance on the one hand and probation officers who seem blindly to ignore the consequences of conditional attendance on the other. Despite the philosophical, political and ethical arguments that will continue, pragmatic considerations will inevitably affect approaches to resolving these dilemmas in practice.

In setting up a project for serious and persistently delinquent juvenile offenders my criteria for selection were based on the *deeds*, not the needs of the offender. Use of a formal condition was thus restricted to those whose deeds (that is their degree of offending) would lead to a custodial sentence – inevitably a small group. By adopting this criterion we avoided the risks attendant upon professional judgements where disposals on grounds of need have led to draconian measures of compulsory care or detention (Thorpe *et al.*, 1980). We required attendance on three evenings a week, for four months for one and a half hour sessions. My experience of running such groups was, on the whole, a good one both in terms of 'rescuing' juveniles from custody and positive feedback from the clients themselves. However one of my continuing concerns about this kind of project, of which there are many others in the intermediate treatment field (now also being done with adult offenders) is whether such conditions are wholly necessary: 'The demand for conformity is sometimes consciously used as treatment technique ... at a more sub-conscious level by group leaders who, invaded by anxiety, may retreat behind the defences of control and authoritarianism' (McCaughan, 1978, p.25). As changes in the political climate have produced a 'coercive tilt' (Walker and Beaumont, 1981) the abuse of such conditions has become much more likely. Decisions need to be made about the degree of compulsion which can be justified recognising that even the 'traditional' statutory court orders contain conditions and therefore some coercion through the threat of sanctions.

Many groups do operate broadly within a statutory framework even though attendance may not be a specific requirement of an order. Encouragement to attend groups should always be offered in an open atmosphere accepting that for some the reality can feel like Hobson's choice. Certainly to elect to attend groups whilst under supervision can never be a completely free choice. Heap (1977) talks of the notion of 'pseudo-voluntary groups'. He uses this term to indicate the pressure that individuals often feel to attend a group recommended by a probation officer, particularly when the alternatives may seem bleak or damning. For instance prisoners may feel it will do their parole prospects some good if they attend a particular pre-release group, and conversely may jeopardise their chances if they choose not to attend even when no overt pressure is applied. This is not only a problem for institutional groups but also for community-based work such as alcohol education and drug rehabilitation.

Specific extra conditions present particular problems. A considerable degree of criticism has been directed at projects and programmes operating on a groupwork basis whose primary and overriding rationale is containment, control and surveillance. We have to address the degree of constraint compatible with the elements of the socialist approach developed below. There can be no precise or neat answer. Critical awareness of whether requirements are wholly necessary, whether they fundamentally conflict with the aims of the group and whether they have been instituted merely to allay the fears of the worker concerning structure and order need to be part of the debate. Individual socialists will come to different decisions, but we cannot ignore the fact that we work 'in and against the state', whether we eschew extra conditions or not. Stone (1981) highlights an important dimension in suggesting that there comes a point, quite evident in penal institutions, where the degree and nature of controls imposed make effective provision of help a forlorn hope as borstal regimes have proved. This discussion has been necessarily cursory. I would assert, however that for a small group of offenders when there is a clear threat of a custodial sentence on the *offence* criterion alone there can be some limited value in groups with a condition of attendance. Additional conditions in probation orders pose crucial problems but their use in groupwork can be limited to the category of offender described above. Most offenders can have a more open choice and we need to maximise that potential wherever possible.

## Socialist style

Recognising the limitations imposed by the legal context does not preclude working towards an authentic and coherent personal practice which is congruent with a socialist political philosophy. Walker and Beaumont (1981) rightly eschew the search for a radical method. However by emphasising certain elements of practice it is possible to develop an approach I would term a *socialist style* which can enhance the potential for achieving worthwhile practice in the use of groups. Many of these aspects are obviously not peculiar to the socialist and thus are shared characteristics of many groupworkers. However through awareness of the benefits of stressing such aspects we can seek to develop a prefigurative form of socialist groupwork.

### Reducing individualism

Walker and Beaumont (1981) detailed the tendency of the criminal justice system and the probation service to individualise problems. Working with a group of people is potentially a way of countering this, by operating on a range of issues without treating them solely or necessarily as problems centred in, or peculiar to, the individuals involved. Individuals within groups often begin to discover that their perceptions of problems are transformed or altered when shared with other group members. Two potential advantages flow from working in a group. There are possibilities for mutual support to develop, as I discuss below. Secondly it creates an environment where a whole range of attitudes and solutions to problems can be rehearsed. This creates a real opportunity for a group to set goals to pursue which might be fundamentally different to each individual's choice of goals when reflecting on their own. Two examples from practice will demonstrate this potential.

Social skills work with groups of offenders can help them to tackle problems. The lack of particular skills such as coping with interviews, use of the telephone, form-filling and knowledge of welfare rights is commonly recognised by many offenders. Often learning such skills is a relatively easy task and has undoubted benefits and use to offenders. However, resistance can stem from the feeling that everyone else has these skills which they alone lack. Working within groups can reveal that each individual has different skills which can be shared in a learning situation. In turn the resistance to personal skill development may be reduced. Many offenders go to great lengths to conceal problems such as basic literacy which inhibit effective social functioning. Rarely are all group members faced with the same problem – a pooling of existing knowledge and sharing of skill has side benefits like an increase in confidence and self-esteem.

Unemployment creates feelings of guilt and personal inadequacy. Working with groups of unemployed offenders can enable them to consider alternative perceptions of the same dilemma and connections can be made to wider social and political circumstances. This is possible in individual work but only through the particular promptings of the officer. Group-work does not depend on the officer for such connections to be made; they can arise spontaneously through the members' interaction. The effect on perceptions of problems is not confined to clients. I recall inviting an educational welfare officer to discuss truanting with a group of adolescents. Whilst an isolated youth might have found difficulty convincing the authorities that school was irrelevant and oppressive, the group expressing such views and gaining confidence through supporting each other had a significant impact on the visitor.

Working with groups is not tantamount to neglecting each individual and his or her personal needs. It is important to remember that airing common problems can generate power-ful and anxiety-provoking feelings. Indeed one of the real risks of working with groups is the exposure, scapegoating and isolation that members can experience. There are ways to minimise these risks through sensitive leadership and by ensuring continuing individual support. If the group is not structured towards individual exposure or behaviour change then this acts as a further safeguard, allowing participants to make their own decisions as to when to take part and what to reveal. Individuals often feel support and benefit by simply being in the group and listening to views being expressed by others.

### Choice over participation

In view of the legal context in which we operate it would appear that any discussion about choice is somewhat illusory. However, two prescriptions for practice are worth emphasis-ing. Firstly groups for mutual support – women's groups, community-based groups for local adolescents or groups which spring naturally from a particular setting such as day centres or probation hostels – can be voluntary in a real sense. Typically these groups operate outside the legal framework although some participants may be on a statutory order but choosing to attend. Characteristically they are self-directed, loose-knit, open-ended and serve many purposes – support, self-help, learning, sharing, discussion and simply social chat. The probation officer's role is important, but limited to encouraging or facilitating group formation – finding a building, getting resources, inviting potential members to attend, acting as a personal resource for the group, organising speakers, getting transport for visits, responding to personal problems. Crucially attendance is not determined by officer direction. A wider cross-section of the community may be able and willing to participate than is the case if the group is restricted to identified offenders or statutory clients. Working in this way with a group of juvenile offenders in a mining village enabled me to meet with their wider peer group and construct activities useful to them. Such groups are an important and valuable service and we should resist attempts to lessen or devalue their impact. They are chaotic, unpredictable, stimulating and if members gain on their terms from involvement, worth developing.

Secondly, choice over participation is wider than simply whether attendance is voluntary or not. A real chance to influence the content, style and direction of a group can be attempted by open leadership and a commitment to give group members meaningful control. The agenda should not be prescribed by the leader alone. Every opportunity should be pursued to enable the group to direct their energies towards issues defined by them. It must be acknowledged that there is often a high level of compliance and diffidence in any created group but a commitment to involving the participants can, and in my experience does, succeed.

### Self-help and mutual aid

Notions of mutual aid and self-help have had a long history in social work and related fields (McCaughan, 1978). Probation officers have appreciated the possibilities of capitalising on self-help potential, bringing offenders together to share and discuss common concerns. Working in this way with prostitutes, the unemployed, women, black youth or the isolated can bring more confidence, solidarity and a sense of common oppression. In turn this can lead them to a more self-assertive posture. Whitlock working from a probation base, writes how she and her co-workers set up a group for women with the dual aims of encouraging self-help and creating opportunities for the development of educational and social skills. The aspects they felt enabled it to succeed were that it was voluntary, open-ended, programmes were flexible, the women began to own the group and interest was shown by the local courts. The informal setting, she writes, 'resulted in various self-help phenomena as well as a marked improve-ment in the women's social skills' (Whitlock, 1983, p.14).

We can encourage our clients simply to support each other or to take initiatives to work together to tackle issues. To some extent, self-help concepts lie a little uncomfortably with artificial groups initiated by statutory workers with particular individuals in mind. There are real problems of knowing what role the workers might assume. Indeed many self-help groups are extremely distrustful of active participation by profes-sional workers. Nevertheless it remains useful for officers to create opportunities for clients, trapped within their own limited definition of their problems, to meet with similar people for mutual support. This can be enhanced by using existing networks. Feeding into a context in which clients are familiar, for example an adolescent peer-group, can reduce the potential for worker-determined priorities. Clearly, too, it is an aid to self-motivation, as the more control over the group that members can exercise, the more motivation they may come to feel for the total enterprise:

> Group discussion has a great impact on the level of motivation of members of a group. The presence of other people with similar problems which they wish to tackle is a powerful motivating factor for individuals in any learning context. This is a principle that has been exploited by self-help groups ... (Priestley *et al.* 1978, p.84)

### Nature of power relationships

> The cherished one-to-one probation officer/client relationship can be understood as a fetishised form. It is portrayed as containing an element of equality between the two parties ... yet ... at the root of the probation relationship lies a fundamental inequality in power. (Walker and Beaumont, 1981, p.148)

Individual supervisors are in a particularly powerful position in relation to the client, buttressed by authority delegated from the court. Groupwork potentially shifts the balance of power somewhat, by exposing workers to the combined resources of the group members. Any worker who has been subjected to a group of juveniles choosing to disrupt activities, or refusing to be involved, will know how difficult and anxious it can make you feel. However, it is at least an indication that the group feel they can exercise control over the situation.

There are two particular *caveats*. Firstly, groups where attendance is through compulsory requirements have clear limits to the exercise of independent will by group members. Working alongside two youth workers on a compulsory intermediate treatment scheme, I found that my position in the group, whatever my personal style, was perceived differently by the group members. My connection with the court which had directed them there meant that to a degree the juveniles distanced themselves from me and were closer to my co-workers.

A second problem relates simply to the fact that the professional worker is often more confident and articulate and can misuse this expertise to manipulate and thus control the situation. There is a danger of this occurring without you realising it; working with other probation officers can reduce this possibility. The pitfalls mentioned can be avoided both by refusing to play on such power and by working more with self-directed and voluntary groups. It is tempting to retreat behind the comfort of court requirements either to limit the exercise of power by the group or avoid taking a clear and open look at the efficacy of the groupwork undertaken. This should be resisted.

### Democratic leadership

There is an extensive literature on the nature of group leadership which demonstrates that personal style can clearly have a significant effect on the atmosphere of a group. Lippitt and White (1958) examining leadership noted authoritarian, democratic and *laissez-faire* styles, and that group behaviour tended to be consistent with leadership style. The democratic mode tended to encourage group cohesion and harmonious working relationships even when the leader was absent. Clearly a leadership style which enhances a collaborative and shared approach would be congruent with the tenets of groupwork discussed in this chapter. In this style the leader's task is to help the group discover what is useful to them. The precise direction emerges, via negotiation, from the collective endeavour of the group. The leader is particularly employed in a mediating role, supporting people within the group as appropriate. A probation officer, investigating the effectiveness of groups for young offenders, concluded: 'The consensual agreement between the leader and the members in relation to function and purpose is of undoubted importance to the successful functioning of the group' (Leivers, 1980, p.7).

It is hard to achieve democratic leadership. The experience of authority by offenders makes it difficult for them to trust workers adopting such a style of leadership. Nevertheless, it is important to work towards achieving this style. Lippitt and White's research noted that *laissez-faire* leadership achieved little, whether the leader was present or not, and we must guard against simply abdicating any responsibility for group development. As probation officers we carry authority, whether we choose to use it or not. It is important to acknowledge that, while working towards the worthwhile and essential goal of a democratic leadership style.

### Co-working

Given the nature of the criminal justice system, the socialist is constantly in situations where it is easy to compromise or lose sight of basic values and ideology. Working in isolation can potentially inhibit a critical awareness of the effects of our actions on clients. Neither are we in a position to challenge the way others work. Groupwork naturally lends itself to working with colleagues and opening up practice for scrutiny. The problems of racism, sexism or more generally, the development of a correctionalist approach to the offender can be challenged by the observation of one by another. Particularly helpful can be the use of a colleague as a sounding board, to help you reflect on your work in a way which forces you to be more critically aware of underlying attitudes and views. Working with others is demanding, because challenges to your methods and style are potentially very stressful. However if we are constantly to question and be aware of the direction of our practice such scrutiny is vital and should be liberating. Co-working is also a learning process, for it allows you to observe and pick up from others aspects of style and approaches which can enhance your personal practice.

## Using techniques

It is not my intention here to debate the efficacy of role-play, group discussion or experiential learning. I have used a whole range of techniques to achieve the tasks that groups set themselves and feel generally that I have tried to handle the apprehension and reluctance of participants in a sensitive manner. In considering this issue attention should be addressed both to the purpose of techniques and to the ways in which they are introduced. Some intermediate treatment programmes have made use of crude behaviourist techniques intended to fundamentally alter future behaviour patterns. Apart from the limited chance of this succeeding, such a correctional perspective is based on positivistic notions of criminal behaviour and fails to recognise the wider contextual basis of crime – the social construction of deviance.

I cannot suggest a blueprint which avoids the possibility of groups becoming extremely oppressive for individuals. I became aware through experience, feedback and reflection of exercises which can usefully be attempted at particular times. That adolescents keenly ask for video to be introduced, and used, is some testament to their willingness to work with such approaches. As social workers we have responsibilities to engage with our clients and this does involve risk-taking. This is true both for ourselves – we should be prepared to take part in any exercise we wish to use with others – and also for group members – we need to be prepared to challenge their perceptions of their problems. Different methods will be appropriate according to particular circumstances. We must guard against working in ways which are felt as oppressive by the participants. Useful yardsticks when considering specialist methods are those of clients' rights and civil liberties.

## Educational

Many of our clients have had only marginal benefit from the formal educational system. A large number have basic literacy problems to which day-care settings particularly can have a lot to offer. More pertinently for groupwork there are large numbers whose experience of education has been alienating or who, because of other factors (family problems, housing, being put into care or other institutions), have had little opportunity to make positive use of the system. In recent years there has been a debate, particularly in further education, about how adults learn. It is argued that we need to rid ourselves of the pedagogic assumptions of teacher-led, didactic teaching and look to basic learning conditions which start from the position of the learner. This can offer us pointers for the education work we hope to carry out through groupwork.

Jarvis (1983) argues that a 'humanistic basis for education' starts where the learner is rather than where the teacher wishes to begin. Certain characteristics in this analysis are held to underpin the learning process. This includes a recognition that physiological conditions vary amongst individuals and can thus affect ability to learn. The variety of 'educational biographies' adds to the need for a tolerance towards different speeds and styles of learning. Other central elements include encouraging adults to participate actively in learning; ensuring the teacher understands the level of self-perception, self-esteem and confidence of the learner; recognising that adults learn best when not under threat; acknowledging the need for adults to be treated as responsible, autonomous people. (For a fuller discussion see Jarvis, 1983, ch. 1–6). Jarvis recognises that his approach is basically individualistic and phenomenological, but he does point out similarities to the structural and political approach of Freire. He too is concerned with a two-way model of interaction between teacher and learner which is geared to the encouragement of 'education for freedom': Freire (1972) argues that education cannot be regarded as a neutral endeavour but that it has potential to encourage freedom. By this he means freedom from the cultural legacy of the ruling class and he juxtaposes traditional 'education for domestication' which is basically conservative. The tenets that underpin Jarvis' approach to adult learning would be echoed by Freire.

Given the context within which learning should take place, it is possible to envisage groups quite deliberately using their time together to pursue educational work. It is a neglected but important task for the probation officer. Formal education courses, such as Open University short courses, if attempted in the conditions of learning described above, could well lead to educational experiences being successfully undertaken rather than further alienation. Basic learning may too be a prerequisite for other problems to be understood and articulated. Probation officers can look with profit at developments in adult education.

## The personal and the political

The previous sections have concentrated on process rather than content and have suggested certain elements which, if enhanced and encouraged, will reduce the dissonance that socialist probation officers may feel when working with offenders. This final section makes some tentative suggestions about approaching personal problems and difficulties in a way which locates solutions in a wider political and economic context. Groupwork is a useful vehicle for this approach.

A small group focus in the 1960s in both women's groups and in 'new left' movements stressed a lack of formal structure, emphasis on participation and sharing of tasks. Similar elements have been emphasised here within the restrictions of the legal context of probation groupwork. In the same period, particularly in the women's movement, attempts were made to see the reality of everyday life in a different way, in short to raise consciousness of the nature of oppression. The slogan 'the personal is the political' became a way of naming this process and I believe socialist group workers might benefit from viewing their enterprise through the insights of this critical period for the women's movement.

Probation officers deal daily with a range of individual

problems which I have suggested can often be more profitably tackled in a groupwork setting. However, it is important to focus on such personal problems in a way which illuminates the oppressed position that many clients are in, rather than merely locate solutions in an evaluation of their present problems (though such tasks should not be excluded). Two connected beliefs underpin the feminist notion of the 'personal is the political'. Firstly the essential validity of personal experience must be acknowledged. Secondly the traditional distinction between the 'objective' and the 'subjective' is a false dichotomy – the subjective nature of experience being central to examining political dimensions. Through examining and sharing experiences of the family, work, educational system and so on this approach 'emphasises that "the system" is experienced in everyday life, and isn't separate from it' (Stanley and Wise, 1983, p.53). In addition 'From this group sharing comes the realisation that what traditionally has been seen as "personal problems" in fact have social and political bases and solutions' (ibid., 1983, p.54). Seemingly complex analytical issues such as power and its use can and should be examined within personal situations. Consciousness-raising deliberately locates thinking in everyday experience and arises from the ability to translate those experiences into altered perceptions of the same reality. I am not suggesting that clients have a wrong picture of the world. The idea of false consciousness is dangerously presumptive. It follows from this that I do not think small-group discussions should be fashioned or directed by group leaders. This would contradict the shared nature of groupwork I have previously stressed. I regard it as impossible and mistaken analytically to separate the personal and political dimensions of social experience. Too many radicals, working towards social and political change, make little reference to the everyday realities of unique but vital personal experiences.

Freire offers a different insight in relation to the same dilemma. Examining education, he argues that it cannot be seen as a neutral process and, of necessity, means political activity. He refers to the idea of conscientisation as 'A permanent critical approach to reality in order to discover the myths that deceive us and help to maintain the oppressing dehumanising structures' (Freire, 1976, p.225). Again there is an emphasis on collective discovery and collective actions, on not pre-determining goals but encouraging congruity between personal and political dimensions. The ideas of the women's movement and Freire are far more complex and developed than it is appropriate to discuss here. They have been mentioned because they restore the centrality of personal experience in the context of a political analysis. They illustrate how individual probation officers can and should encourage the sharing of personal experiences, as part of a process which may begin to help our clients to discuss altered perceptions of the world around them. As Davies suggests, in an analysis of Freire, much social skills work has had limited instrumental goals: 'Primarily, they aim to help fulfil basic occupational and social functions – to fill in forms and read shop signs – though they may attempt, too, to enable them to gain certain personal – *individual* – satisfactions. What they lack unmistakably are any explicitly liberating *collective* and *political* purposes' (Davies, 1982, p.181).

Socialist groupworkers need to develop the opportunities to make such links and thus preserve a unity between the personal and political. As Wilson writes in relation to the women's movement:

> Women talk about their experiences and thereby come to understand that their problems which seemed personal to them and part of their individual inadequacy or neurosis are actually a part of the way in which women are defined and oppressed. Group support and strength, gradually formed, leads to more outgoing political activities as well as continued mutal support. (Wilson, 1980, p.36).

# 8

# Day Centres

Paul James

During the past decade day centres have been one of the growth areas within the probation service, although as yet little has been written about them. Within the probation service there are many different kinds of centres. My own experience has been in a voluntary centre linked to the service, but not reliant upon it for either accommodation or funding. Throughout the chapter my aim will be to give an overall impression of day centres, with particular focus on the work, and type of centre with which I am involved.

## Day centre development

Probation service involvement with day centres began, on a national scale, with the introduction of the Criminal Justice Act 1972. Prior to this some experimentation had taken place with drop-in centres, but on a limited and localised basis. The provisions of the Act were consolidated in the Powers of the Criminal Court Act 1973 and pilot experiments were established in four areas – Liverpool, London, Pontypridd and Sheffield. The legal framework within which the centres operated was contained in Section 4 of the 1973 Act. It included conditions in the probation order that the person should attend for not more than 60 days, and whilst attending should comply with instructions given at the centre. Initially the centres were aimed at 'socially inadequate offenders' whose repeated offending was supposed to be linked with an inability to cope with everyday pressures. The centres operated along therapeutic lines, until social skills courses became popular.

At the same time interest in the concept grew in other areas, and centres were established outside of the Act. The Barbican Centre for instance, opened in 1973, was based on voluntary attendance and attempted to link its work with a variety of local groups. By the mid 1970s day centres and drop-in centres were mushrooming in a number of areas. Day centres initially faced the accusation that they were taking people out of the labour market, but with the subsequent rise in unemployment this objection was largely removed. The increase in the number of centres coincided with, and must to some extent be connected to the rise of unemployment. However, the response of probation areas to unemployment varied enormously. Some ignored it completely, while others offered provisions ranging from a room in an office building, open for half a day each week, to varied activities five days a week in a specially equipped building. In most cases attendance was voluntary.

With the advent, in the late 1970s, of a reactionary 'new right' doctrine and an emphasis on more coercive measures, the change in attitude from treatment to control was accelerated. In response some day centres began to offer what they considered to be an alternative to imprisonment; a condition of attendance in probation orders, often including a structured programme of treatment and containment. The Home Office Research Unit (1981, p.26) concluded that 'Day centres can constitute a direct alternative to prison, perhaps via statutory orders, where a structured formal programme is available.' In the early 1980s, with unemployment rising to over three million, day centres appeared to offer a direct response both to unemployment and increasing crime figures. Over eighty were in operation, and at one stage new centres were being opened at the rate of one a month (Burney, 1980, pp. 1–2). Even at this stage some areas did not understand the structural nature of unemployment, and were still concerned with improving users' chances of employment through development of good work habits.

A Home Office Research Unit Paper (1981, pp. 4–5)

classified centres into six categories according to purpose, and I have used this to provide a guide to the range of provision:

1.  Alternative to Custody: such centres had to demonstrate their ability to control their users and intervention was likely to be intensive.
2.  Alternative to traditional probation methods: these encompass aims such as rehabilitation, prevention of further offending and fostering self-help.
3.  Employability: these are concerned with teaching social skills and sometimes practical skills such as timekeeping and respect for tools.
4.  Educative: they aim to provide remedial educational, literacy and numeracy training, concentrating on the acquisition of practical skills.
5.  Socialisation: these described their work as rehabilitation and concentrated on helping users conform better to society's norms.
6.  Containment: in preference to trying to change users, these centres merely set out to provide a place to go. Whilst clients are there they are not on the streets where they could get into trouble or be a nuisance.

The Criminal Justice Act 1982 abolished the Day Training Centre but paradoxically introduced the 'Day Centre'. The decision in the House of Lords in *Rogers v. Cullen* (1982), where attendance at a centre, other than a Day Training Centre, by means of inserting a requirement in the probation order to attend was held to be unlawful, was overturned by the Act. Courts are now able to order attendance for up to 60 days, so long as they have consulted the probation officer, arranged for attendance and secured the client's consent. A day centre in this Act means premises at which non-residential facilities are provided for use in connection with the rehabilitation of offenders, and which have been approved or provided by the probation committee. A possible consequence of the Act is that Home Office-financed day centres may now be pressed to offer attendance as a condition of orders to local courts.

## Unemployment and day centres

Probation day centres, voluntary or compulsory, are by nature used by the unemployed simply because those in work are not free to attend. Probation case-loads throughout the country have a large proportion of unemployed clients and probation officers deal, in the main, with an age group particularly vulnerable to unemployment – seventeen- to twenty-four-year olds – so involvement in provision could be seen as essential. The West Midlands Probation Service Research Unit have said that, in 1982, between 70 and 80 per cent of all clients were unemployed. This compares with a general rate for the area of about 18 per cent. As unemployment has risen, so the number of long-term unemployed has grown more rapidly. According to Manpower Services Commission (1983) figures, up to 60 per cent of those out of work have been unemployed for anything between one and three years. The Unemployment Unit (1982) state that long-term unemployment is increasingly affecting the younger age group, so that although in the 1960s and 1970s the majority were over 45 years old, now 60 per cent are under that age and the fastest growth is among the under 25s. Most long term unemployed are semi- or unskilled although the professional section is now the area which is growing most rapidly. Women, the disabled and ethnic minorities are the worst hit, although women are less visible because they tend to be confined within the home.

The effects of unemployment on individuals and families is demoralising and destructive. Hedges and Benyon (1982) encapsulate its significance: 'Unemployment affects everyone. It affects those in work and those out of work. It affects your horizons, how you think about things and how you plan, what you'll put up with, what you'll complain about and what you'll let pass' (p.87) and 'it's the weak who suffer most – the young, the old and sick, black people and women. If you have a vulnerability the system will find it' (p.90). Day-centre provision is one part of the service's reaction to the problem of unemployment and resources have been channelled into a wide range of day/drop-in centres. In the face of massive unemployment there seems little point in maintaining the emphasis, common in probation practice, on enforcing the work ethic and discipline. Yet some probation projects continue to operate regimes designed to return clients to the job market. A tension remains about what realistically can or should be done when unemployment is so high. Courses and workshops have been established to guide probation officers' thinking when setting up a centre and a variety of ideas has become apparent. For instance the Midlands Regional Staff Development booklet takes the view that 'A variety of people using a provision not only tends to reduce the stigma on our clients but also helps to integrate members of the community' (Purser *et al.*, 1982, p.8). On the other hand, the Leicestershire Probation Service (1983) describe a highly structured day centre:

> The day centre provides intensive supervision in the community by means of educational and recreational activities in a structured environment . . . while attending, instructions given by, or under the authority of, the day centre's probation officers must be complied with . . . these will include instructions to participate in educational and recreational activities, both in the centre and at other places.

At the present time, the majority of day centres tend not to be so directive or authoritarian as the Leicestershire model, but the Criminal Justice Act 1982 may lead to a shift. Those working in centres have to be clear how they can work with and assist unemployed users.

### Conditions or voluntary attendance?

> 'Structure irons out uncertainties but it may discriminate against some users.' (Howe *et al.*, 1982, p.61)

The issue of control and conditions within the probation order has been the subject of debate within the probation service and NAPO for some time, but was heightened by the provisions within the Criminal Justice Act 1982. It is an issue which is crucial for a day centre because it can and does influence the manner of operation. Differences of opinion exist among socialist probation officers regarding conditions of attendance at centres. Some have worked in Day Training

Centres, or are involved in centres now using conditions, but have been able to reconcile themselves to that way of working and still point to results. These workers are aware of, and able to cope with, the natural distrust and conflict which arises from the need to enforce attendance, but feel that if the rules are explained clearly they tend to be accepted by clients. Those who work in these centres assert that conditions do not stop the involvement of other clients on a voluntary basis. Some workers have said that on occasions they feel like community prison officers, but they believe this tension applies to all probation officers, to a greater or lesser extent. In a field office it may be easier to forget or manage that difficulty. Within a day centre the control role can easily affect the way you work; for instance there is a possibility of adopting an over-rigid style because of the relationship between the centre and the court.

I personally agree with those who oppose conditions of attendance at day centres. There is little value in providing useful services for offenders and then attaching conditions of attendance or obedience to instructions. Whilst recognising the possible appeal this type of order could have for the courts, we should consider the impact on the workers and users. Day-centre workers have to ensure that the condition is observed and are thus placed in a position of control. Users are subject to direct constraints which entail a substantial curtailment of their civil liberties. If attendance is voluntary, people attend because they want to, because they feel there is something to be gained. They will continue to attend if the centre is felt to be worthwhile and of value. It is then the centre which responds to the needs of the users and the community, not the user who is tailored to meet the needs of the centre. If both offenders and others from the community are taking part in activities, stigmatisation and isolation may be minimised. There is more likelihood of users achieving limited goals if they are not under compulsion to take part in activities which they see as being of little value. Their attainments are then shared by users and workers alike; because they have not occurred through compulsion the satisfaction and achievement will be greater and have more lasting effect. With voluntary participation it is possible for users to be actively involved in decision making and the day-to-day operation of the centre, thus ensuring satisfaction gained from a co-operative effort.

It is difficult to see what positive advantages can be gained for a day centre by the insertion of conditions in a probation order. Acceptance of these conditions does not meet the needs of the user or the community and may simply be succumbing to the pressures for coercive measures. The unemployed are oppressed by both perceived and actual status, and further controls only worsen their situation.

## Limitations and potential

It is tempting, when talking to an enthusiastic proponent of day centres, to believe that such provision can be a panacea for all ills, but clearly this is not the case. It is an area full of potential, particularly for a socialist, but as with any method of work which has its roots in the statutory field there are limitations which need to be recognised. In this section some of the limitations and potential of day-centre work will be examined.

Some limitations on useful progressive practice may arise in centres with a rigidly structured regime. Centres closely connected with the probation service; dependent on probation funding, and catering just for offenders will be more likely to suffer this limitation. Some probation officers may find it easier to operate in this kind of setting because of the defined limits and greater clarity of role. However more community-based centres will offer socialist probation officers greater opportunity for working in a flexible, imaginative and useful way. This will widen the scope of the probation service response to unemployment and offending.

Another limitation encountered in probation service funded day centres is that they may find themselves short of users because they set themselves strict criteria for referral: 'Almost all day centres, and all day training centres have at one time or another suffered from the referrals problem and most continue to do so. It can get to a point where the facilities are so under-used as to destroy the validity of the whole enterprise (Burney, 1980, p.42). More community-oriented centres which accept a broader-based and self-referring clientele are likely to be better used, thus maximising the use of resources.

Within a day centre a considerable amount of time is spent with the users in groups, informal discussions or carrying out activities together. This increased contact and informality may enable relationships to develop quickly and allow helpful work to be carried out. However a contradiction of all probation work is also present in day-centre work – clients may still be resistant to our influence because of our authority role as probation officers (Walker and Beaumont, 1981). Day-centre work however may minimise this barrier and allow more meaningful discussions and work with clients to take place.

A day centre has the potential to make contacts in the local community, thus offering a broader approach and enabling the sharing of resources. For example, a day centre could make links with an unemployment centre operated by a Trades Council offering welfare and benefit advice. This could provide users with greater opportunities for stimulation and constructive alternatives to the boredom and frustration which unemployment can bring. They can also develop a sense of belonging and solidarity which assists in breaking down the distinction between clients and the rest of the working class. Implicit in this is the assumption that the centre workers are committed to real involvement with working-class problems and are willing to forgo some loss of autonomy in establishing community and self-help networks.

Having a centre available to the local community brings many benefits and opens avenues which a statutory centre may find difficult to explore. The centre with which I am involved has a room which is frequently used by an Asian Women's Group. In addition to providing the women with a resource, everyone can benefit from the contact with a different culture and can share for instance, cooking and music. The presence of women can be important because probation day centres tend to be male dominated and the input that a women's group can make will not only heighten political education but also encourage women to use the centre.

Day centres have the potential to offer really useful services to clients; warmth, shelter, food, hot drinks, practical advice, recreational and educational activities, groups and counselling. All these services can be offered in ways which users will not find stigmatising or demeaning. However the provision of attractive and useful day-centre facilities poses a problem. It may simply become ' a place to go', encouraging dependency rather than giving users help and support to move on. This is a particular danger at a time of high unemployment and diminishing educational and training opportunities. Workers may then be faced with the problem of whether to plan a regime that simply helps people to cope with unemployment.

Both statutory and voluntary centres produce much more extensive contact between probation officers and their clients than is usual. This is not an unmitigated benefit for clients as it provides for a greater degree of surveillance and can alter the way the client is viewed. There may be difficulties concerning the confidentiality of information accumulated and day-centre workers could find themselves asked to supply, or tempted to volunteer, sensitive information to probation officers or other statutory agencies. The problem will be more acute in centres using conditions where surveillance may lead to breach action. Day-centre workers need to be constantly alert to these dangers. This extensive contact, together with the closer and more informal nature of relationships developed in day-centre work, can also prove problematic for probation officers. Workers have nowhere to hide, many aspects of their behaviour and personality are open to scrutiny and they are therefore more vulnerable. They may experience difficult conflicts of loyalty and these relationships can also be confusing for clients.

It is possible for a centre to be probation service linked but to have its own voluntary management committee and resources. This provides greater potential for links with local groups and response to local issues than would a purely service-based resource where such contacts may be considered outside its brief. A community based centre may also offer the opportunity to work in a co-operative, non-hierarchical manner which can provide a model for socialist ways of working and organising. The sharing of resources can bring close contact with women's groups, black organisations and trade unions. Pressure groups can be assisted, or formed quickly in response to local needs, and it is easy to pass on knowledge, ideas and experience. Co-operatives can be initiated within the centre, assistance can be given with resources; rooms made available for planning or meetings; and support and encouragement given until the group feels able to move on. A word of caution however – there are real limitations on what you can do politically in your role as probation officer. This will vary from area to area but must always be borne in mind. It's no use winning a battle if you are then in no position to continue the war!

## Practice issues

Although it is possible to categorise day centres it should be remembered that there are as many differences as there are centres. As a result there is no blueprint for establishing and running a centre. Development depends on many factors such as locality, buildings and finance available, pressures from management, team and community. A useful guide to the basics of day-care provision was issued by the Midland Region Staff Development Office (Purser *et al.*, 1982). What follows however are some general comments applicable to either an existing centre or one about to be established.

### Finance

The funding of any type of provision always proves a major headache and day centres are no exception, apart perhaps from statutory, service-funded projects. Adequate finance is essential if a major proportion of time and effort is not to be concentrated on fund raising. However the major sources of finance may have conditions attached which can create problems. Monies supplied by the Home Office do not necessarily, but may in future because of the Criminal Justice Act 1982, carry conditions that funding is only available purely for offender-based centres. Some funds are available from the

Home Office for voluntary projects, but these need to be supported by the probation service and, although not exclusively for clients, will have to include a significant number. Funding from service budgets is most likely to be for offender-based projects and the arguments for community-based resources may be more difficult to win. Urban Aid funding is attractive, and enables a centre to be financially secure for at least five years but the application needs a sponsor, usually the local authority or the probation service. Charities are an obvious source of finance but it may take numerous applications before one is successful.

The last major area of funding is the Manpower Services Commission under the Community Programme. At first sight the CP can seem attractive and it must be admitted that many day centres would not be in operation now had it not been for the financial backing of MSC. There is no doubt that past schemes, such as the Community Enterprise Programme, were seen as a legitimate source of funding and so aided the development and progress of many centres which otherwise would not have left the drawing board. However, there are fundamental objections to CP which have been identified in numerous recent papers (for example Salmon, 1983; Unemployment Unit, 1982) and socialists must consider whether MSC schemes operate in the long-term interest of the working class or of the capitalist state. If we implement these schemes in day centres we are in danger of encouraging the depression of wages, the continuation of political expediency and the further exploitation of the working class. Like other trades unions, NAPO (1983b) has adopted a policy which seeks to limit and discourage the service's use of MSC schemes.

Apart from political objections there are a number of practical points which need to be taken into account if it is decided there is more to gain from taking part in the scheme than attempting to obtain funding elsewhere. The Unemployment Unit (1982) makes the point that at £60 per week the only people who can be better off on a scheme are single people living at home or unemployed women not entitled to benefit. Other people will have to claim housing benefit, supplementary benefit or Family Income Supplement. If we intend to employ workers under this scheme it is incumbent on us to provide information to potential workers about the disadvantages they may suffer by taking the job. Information should be obtained and supplied regarding the benefits to which a worker may be entitled. There is also a responsibility on sponsors to balance full and part-time places:

> If a sponsor had one person working full time at £92.50 per week and another person working part-time at £27.50 per week thus maintaining the £60 average and the part-time worker left, then as things stand at the moment, the sponsor or managing agency would be in a position of having to find the difference between £60 and £92.50 for the remaining worker. (Salmon, 1983, p.32)

Objections to CP schemes cannot be discussed fully here for lack of space. I would advise workers and sponsors to read the NAPO policy paper carefully. One restriction which could seriously affect a community-based centre is that the MSC insist that projects they fund should not be involved in any political activity. The *Guardian* (23 March 1983) reported that a Sheffield centre was to have its grant withdrawn because it had been represented on, to quote an MSC spokesperson 'one or two demonstrations and marches – that sort of thing'. This limitation could increasingly limit the involvement of MSC-funded centres in local community issues such as housing, DHSS benefits, women's rights and racism. They will become, as a result, circumscribed in philosophy and the range of activities offered.

*Activities*

What a centre will be able to offer may depend on a number of factors; management pressure, what is practically and financially possible, what the workers consider desirable and feasible and what the users require. The practical list of activities in which day centres can become involved is endless and the following is only a sample of what is happening throughout the country; teaching social and practical skills, remedial education, literacy and numeracy training, self-care, debt counselling, sporting activities, libraries, clothing or furniture stores, renewing canal narrow boats, allotments, food co-operatives, art and crafts. There is a need for constant evaluation of what a centre offers; as the users change they may require different facilities. Activities need not only consist of pool or pinball, although initially that may be the only equipment that is required. If facilities are available, presented as attractive, perceived to be useful or at least interesting, they will be used. In the early days of a drop-in centre in which I was involved we had very little equipment and no money so we were forced to improvise. As a result the most successful activity was a weekly discussion group which, although initially slow, proved to be very popular. Topics ranged from DHSS benefits, football, racism and abortion to Northern Ireland. The cost was nil, apart from the chairs – and they were not necessarily used – and we all learned from the experience because of the varying perspectives put forward. The political input in the discussions depends on the topic, but to hear a woman describe her experiences in a male-dominated society or a black woman talk of day-to-day racism and then to follow it by discussion, can only enlarge everyone's political perception.

Workers should not be discouraged if particular activities are not initially well attended. Provided the need for a particular activity has been established, in consultation with the users, the facility will eventually be used. There is often a need to overcome self-consciousness, particularly amongst male users, with certain activities:

> A centre identified that a substantial core of the users were single males, living in bedsit accommodation. Their diet consisted to a large extent of chips and other convenience foods. The centre therefore began a regular budget cookery course which was initially attended by two people. The male users became very macho at the mention of cookery insisting that it was a 'cissy' activity. However the workers persevered and when various appetising smells drifted around the centre other users gradually lost their inhibitions and joined the course.

Another centre involved a community group, the local Campaign against Fascism and Racism, in one of their discussion groups:

> There had been some signs of racism developing among the younger people within the town and in the General Election the National Front had polled over 1500 votes. The need for education was obvious and in response to a request two members of the Campaign brought along

slides to the centre to supplement their talk. The slides concentrated on the British Empire's exploitation of numerous countries, through the slave trade to the further exploitation of immigrant workers, particularly in the 1950s and 1960s. The first meeting was attended by eight people who in spite of encouragement could not be tempted into any type of meaningful discussion. Although this was somewhat discouraging it was decided to try again, with informal discussion initiated by the workers prior to the actual meeting. This time the room was full and the subsequent discussion lasted three hours; a basis was therefore laid for future education.

It is important and useful for a day centre's activities to include regular contact with other community groups. By doing this we become involved in their lives and struggles. We must be aware of the dangers of isolation and the possible stigma that a centre can attract, particularly if it is solely client based. Clients have lives away from the centre or the probation office, they are subject to the same pressure and fears as other members of the community. By involving them in groups which are attempting to tackle relevant issues, we can enable users to seek control over sections of their lives which may otherwise be lost in apathy. By concentrating on integrated community activity we can work together for social change which will affect us all. This involvement can also produce personal benefits for users:

A user at a centre with close links with the Trades Council, was sponsored by them to take part in the 1981 TUC People's March for Jobs. He received encouragement from other users and the workers. Despite inexperience and nervousness it proved to be an exciting, exhilarating and rewarding experience for him. Because of the sense of not being alone, the comradeship and the enthusiastic support along the route of the march, it had a tremendous effect on him and whilst it did not alter his life – he is still unemployed – it has given him a sense of purpose and he has used the experience in other parts of his daily routine. It was also useful for the centre because the local community were made aware that the unemployed are not content to be pushed on one side, shut off from everyday life, but need and want to be involved in socially useful work.

Centres can be used for a wide range of group discussions and it may be that a group initiated within the probation office would prefer a more informal, relaxed atmosphere in which to meet. A day centre in this case could prove ideal. Educational courses can often be linked with the Workers Educational Association and need not take place at the centre, although they often welcome the opportunity to have a resource which would enable them to initiate a minority interest course. In determining the activities provided in centres, probation officers need to decide whether they are primarily concerned with changing probation practice – using methods which appeal to them – or genuinely seeking to meet client and community needs.

### Coping with problems

In a day centre with a mixed age group attention must be given to the integration of the users because it is easy for them to split into age or activity groups. The potential disruption from this is considerable and a structure needs to be developed taking into account general provision and activities. This requires the users' consent and assistance and should be under constant review, with the possibility of being modified when the need arises. If this is not done the competing claims of the two or more sections of users will take up a considerable amount of the workers' time.

Inevitably, at some stage, there will be abuse of the facilities provided and this can take various forms; violence, drunkenness, theft or vandalism. Obviously there is no easy solution for avoiding abuse but the manner in which the centre is operated can affect eventual behaviour and forestall some of the worst excesses. Problems may be less likely to occur in a centre organised on a co-operative basis. If users feel the centre belongs to them they will be concerned to deal with problems that are upsetting its running. It will help if potential problems can be discussed in an open manner so that solutions can be sought before an explosion occurs. To ilustrate this, I give an example of a centre which initially attempted to operate without set rules or procedure in dealing with people who abused the facilities:

> For some time it appeared to work although there were isolated cases of theft and damage. A crisis point was reached when a user, who had received numerous warnings about gambling and intimidation of younger users, was banned from the centre by the workers. The user did not accept this and a scuffle ensued, after angry exchanges. This incident

forced the workers to look again at the whole structure and it was decided that, with the users' assistance, a minimum set of rules and a procedure for dealing with those who broke these rules should be established. The end result was a structure which users and workers could accept and everyone was clear about their responsibilities to each other and to the centre.

Incidents can arise in spite of extensive planning and it is as well to have a good working practice on which to base the response. Again because users change, it may be necessary to constantly review the manner in which the centre operates, involving new users in any changes of procedure.

Support meetings for workers are necessary on a regular basis. Work in a day centre can be demanding and intense and it is easy to become overstretched. Workers will require support not only for personal survival, but also to maintain a constructive, creative and critical analysis of their work. For a probation officer it is also essential that contact is retained both with the office team and NAPO in order not only to secure their continued support and involvement but also to remain in touch with the mainstream of the service.

## In conclusion

It will be obvious from the content of this chapter that I favour the development of voluntary, co-operative day centres. I have enjoyed the experience of working in such a centre and have been fortunate in being able to exercise considerable freedom in this work. Not all day-centre workers will find they have as much room for manoeuvre but, provided the constraints of the agency do not become too restrictive, there is potential for progressive work even in statutory day centres. They provide a setting in which ideas can be tested and put into practice, in ways that would not be possible within the confines of an office. There are, as I have tried to point out, some dangers in day-centre work but do not be deterred; you, as one of the workers, can help to develop your centre along progressive lines and it will be worth the effort!

# 9

# Developing Probation Practice

Bill Beaumont and Hilary Walker

In this concluding section we examine some issues that run through the preceding chapters and then outline some positive potential for developing practice. We begin with the problems for probation officers posed by the 'new right' doctrines outlined in Chapter 1. Every contributor has identified areas in which government policies have a direct impact on their work. The most obvious effects are the falling living standards and diminishing opportunities of clients. Supervision of probationers, helping those released from prison and extending the prospects for women in the community are all severely limited by the material impact of cuts in public spending. Probation work is made more difficult if there is little hope of improving, even marginally, clients' situations. It is harder to identify positives in social enquiry and parole reports when prospects are so limited. However, Chapter 6 identified campaigning as an important activity which can both expose the real hardships currently experienced by clients, and contribute to the struggle for improvements.

Our contributors have also identified the 'new right' ideology as an issue affecting practice. It impinges on every aspect of our work – the messages we give to clients in one-to-one, day-centre and group work; the difficulties of report writing, court duty and prison-based work in a harsh penal climate; the danger of feeding law and order arguments by taking some crimes against women more seriously; and the powerful impact of state initiatives against 'social security scroungers' in Operation Major. Nevertheless we also identify a potential for countering this ideology. For example, Paul Senior has advocated the use of groups to counter individualisation and Bill Beaumont has explained how campaigning work can counter prevailing images (such as 'social security scroungers') by forceful presentation of alternative accounts.

Finally one of the main planks of 'new right' policy, unemployment, affects probation practice since most clients are without work. Our contributors have identified ways of dealing with this issue without demeaning or demoralising those suffering as a result of government economic strategy. Kevin Kirwin has identified a straightforward helping role, where probation officers do whatever they can to alleviate material hardship and don't nag clients about getting work or joining MSC schemes. Paul James examines the role of day centres in supporting and encouraging the unemployed. He stresses the value of making links in the community both in reducing isolation and raising awareness. Margaret Powell has advocated probation officers injecting the reality of unemployment into the court room. In every area of practice, probation officers should struggle to avoid becoming part of the 'new right' approach to policing and disciplining the unemployed.

## Conditions in probation

One difference in thinking between contributors concerns the use of additional requirements in probation orders. In Chapter 7, Paul Senior supports, with some reservations, a highly selective use of conditions if such use represents a genuine alternative to custody for serious offenders. In Chapter 8, Paul James concedes that some socialists have felt able to work constructively with conditions but argues that their use inhibits progressive work and that there is no value in conditional attendance at day centres. This difference is between two positions (by no means the extremes of the argument) in a long-running and intense debate within the probation service on the use of additional conditions. This controversy represents part of an important struggle over the future direction of the probation service. It would be easy for the service to drift into the routine use of additional and oppressive conditions,

significantly changing the role of the probation officer towards surveillance and containment goals.

Discussion on this issue must recognise that the basic
probation order (88 per cent of all those made in 1982)
contains conditions backed by sanctions. Although these
have generally been viewed as a minimal framework for
contact, they do nevertheless imply a degree of coercion.
Even where requirements are not explicitly enforced probationers may feel pressure to conform to their probation
officers' requests. The two traditional and most commonly
used additional conditions, mental treatment (4 per cent) and
hostel residence (5 per cent) represent a more extensive
curtailment of the probationer's freedom than many newer
requirements. That they have until recently been uncon-
troversial does not mean that they can be ignored in the
debate. Three factors have led to escalating concern about the
use of conditions – the consistent suggestion that the probation service should develop their use into a system of 'control
in the community' (see for example the Younger Report,
1974); developments within the probation service which have
emphasised narrow containment goals; and an increased
emphasis on prohibitive conditions (thou shalt not . . .).

Probation officers have to decide what constitutes acceptable practice recognising the need to provide alternatives to
*real* threats of imprisonments, the danger of drifting into
'routine' use of conditions and problems of inconsistency –
why refuse to use conditions in day centres if you are prepared
to recommend conditions demanding residence at a hostel?
The following guidelines may be useful:

1.  Make minimum use of conditions – always ask first, why
    can't this be done on the basis of a voluntary agreement?
2.  Conditions should not be used in response to 'need'
    criteria – the only justification can be that the client's
    offences would otherwise place them in real danger of
    imprisonment.
3.  Work to ensure that conditions are used only where you
    believe that they are *essential* to persuade a court that an
    offender can be dealt with in the community.
4.  Conditions should be used only when they relate to
    facilities which have a constructive purpose – they should

be resisted when they enable probation to be used as a penalty, prohibit certain activities or give probation officers unfettered discretion.

5. Conditions should impose the minimum feasible infringement of the offender's civil liberties.

6. The condition, and how it will be operated, should be clearly understood and require consent.

Application of these guidelines would encourage continued resistance to the drift towards greater use of conditions and could help in the defence and growth of voluntary facilities. It could lead to more sparing use of existing conditions; less enforced residence at probation hostels might allow them to be used more flexibly for people who choose to live temporarily in such a setting.

These guidelines also provide a framework for critical involvement with projects which use conditions. We need to develop a dialogue with colleagues involved in such work and seek to influence the planning and operation of these schemes. This can sometimes lead to significant modifications and even the abandonment of the use of conditions. Socialist probation officers have found scope for progressive practice when working in day training centres and hostels. This can help to ensure good constructive practice within facilities and minimise restrictions – the Pontypridd Day Training Centre interpreted 60 days attendance to mean 60 mornings and operated as a voluntary day centre in the afternoon. Where hostels operate rules about when residents should be in at night, staff can ensure that these are flexible, not unduly restrictive, fairly operated and that breach action only follows the giving of warnings and opportunities for explanation. Throughout this book the stress has been on finding the balance between limitations and potential; the same approach can be applied in considering the use of conditions in probation orders.

**The personal and the political**

A consistent theme of this book has been the connections between personal attitudes, experiences, circumstances and political understanding. Paul Senior argued that it is mistaken to try to analyse or understand personal problems outside the political dimension of social experience. He suggested that groupwork is a useful way of guiding the process of obtaining a political grasp of personal issues and a personal appreciation of the political dimension. However this thread can be identified throughout the whole book. Because many of the problems faced by our clients are socially and politically constructed – unemployment, poverty, homelessness, imprisonment – it is impossible to gain a holistic understanding of their situation without a grasp of political issues.

It is, however, easier to make these connections than it is to work on them. Probation officers have traditionally been expected to focus on personal solutions, and political matters are often thought to be beyond their brief. We would argue that this separation is false and that dealing with issues labelled 'political' is inevitable. Kevin Kirwin has found that, when talking with clients, it is useful to try and point out the similarities between offenders and other working-class people and in this way political connections are raised. Paul James has described how, for male day-centre users, listening to a black woman talk about her personal experience of racism enlarged political understanding. From these examples it seems clear that there are many useful opportunities to make personal/political connections in daily practice. In this way we can counteract the individualised focus of probation work. Campaigning work also offers a way forward. By becoming an integral part of probation officers' work it can provide a means to achieve a synthesis in our practice between the personal and the political. The Oxford probation officers both helpfully dealt with the plight of those arrested during Operation Major, and highlighted the political nature of the exercise. The 'personal and the political' remains an area in which practice needs to be developed through testing out what is both realistic and possible, through debate amongst probation officers, within teams and in the union.

### Practice potential

In *Probation Work* we identified some broad guidelines for a progressive, socialist probation practice. The various contributions in this book have looked in greater detail at particular areas of probation work and have consolidated, developed and enlarged those practice prescriptions. Here we pick out some common elements which, in our view, have more general application. We all found useful the idea of *socialist style*. This was used to identify both the particular features of the groupwork method which have positive potential and ways in which that potential can be maximised. Other contributors have moved towards identifying a 'socialist style' in court work, day centres and work with prisoners. We think the same general approach can be used in constructing positive practice in other tasks, social-work methods and in response to dilemmas encountered.

Kevin Kirwin emphasises the importance of *open and honest* relationships with clients in individual work – this is an easy principle to support formally but, as he points out, it has far-reaching practice implications. Other contributors stress this approach in writing court reports, involving clients in campaigning and resisting the pressures experienced in working in courts and prisons. It includes being honest about the limits to the help which can be delivered in practice. All the chapters have placed *help to clients* as a central purpose in a socialist approach to probation work. Nigel Stone advocates the *development of useful services* for prisoners and others argue for similar developments for defendants before the courts, women in the criminal justice system and users in day centres. Hilary Walker draws attention to the importance of making *positive provision for disadvantaged groups* – the probation service must not reinforce the discrimination encountered by women. Although not directly dealt with in this book, several contributors touch on the need for special provision by the probation service for black people. Prisoners are also identified as a group specifically disadvantaged by their incarceration and therefore in need of positive provision.

Paul Senior emphasises the potential in groupwork for *educational help* and considers lessons which the probation service can learn from the field of adult education, including the need for teaching methods which are neither didactic nor patronising. Other contributors discuss ways in which prisoners and day-centres users can take advantage of educational opportunities. The importance of educational work with colleagues and within the agency is also raised in connection with tackling sexist attitudes and improving social enquiry report practice. Paul James stresses the potential in day centres for *developing community involvement* and the positive results this can produce. The same advantage is identified in groupwork, and good links with community groups are seen as a crucial need in work with prisoners. These community links can lead to a joint involvement in campaigning. This is identified by Bill Beaumont as an approach which can expose injustices and social problems to critical debate. Other contributors identify potential for *campaigning* in court work, individual practice and in work with prisoners.

Most contributors have commented, in different ways, on the strength to be drawn from *collective work*. Margaret Powell acknowledges the limitations of court teams but still supports a teamwork approach. Others point to the potential of co-working in groupwork, joint involvement in campaigning and the need for honesty between colleagues. In the face of difficult problems and adverse changes, socialists can find mutual support and creative collaboration in collective approaches. Such co-operation needs to be stretched beyond the immediate team to collective work and action through the union. Several contributors have stressed the importance of wider links with socialists in other spheres. We need to be prepared to learn from the struggles of others and to use information from those fields to inform our practice.

In our introduction we identified further deterioration in the social and political context of practice since we wrote *Probation Work* in 1980. Nevertheless we think the contributors to this book have been able to identify continued potential for progressive practice and have enlarged our prescriptions for a socialist approach in probation work. The pressures on the probation service have been real and considerable, but the fightback from probation officers has been worthwhile and effective. In the present climate it is easy to retreat into cynical detachment or fatalistic defeatism. A recognition of the considerable problems faced requires instead a determined defence and pursuit of basic socialist principles in our probation work. Persistence is needed to defend against oppressive encroachments, to provide useful help to clients, to resist and expose injustices and to exploit opportunities for constructive developments. The evidence provided by our contributors is that the potential for progressive probation work has so far been defended and that vital work remains to be done.

# References

Attlee, C. (1920) *The Social Worker*, Bell quoted in J. R. Cypher, 'Social Reform and the Social Work Profession', in H. Jones (ed.) (1975) *Towards a New Social Work*, London, Routledge & Kegan Paul.

Barclay Report (1982) *Social Workers: Their Role and Tasks*, London, Bedford Square Press.

Barrett, M. and McIntosh, M. (1982) *The Anti-Social Family*, London, Verso.

BASW (1977) *The Social Work Task*, Birmingham.

Beauvoir, S. de (1974) *The Second Sex*, Harmondsworth, Penguin.

Bottoms, A. E. and McWilliams, W. (1979) 'A Non-Treatment Paradigm for Probation Practice', *British Journal of Social Work*, vol. 9, no. 2.

Box-Grainger, J. (1982a) 'RAP – A New Strategy?', *The Abolitionist*, no. 3.

Box-Grainger, J. (1982b) *Sentencing Rapists*, London, RAP.

Brittan, L. (1984) Address to the Parliamentary All-Party Penal Affairs Group (21 February 1984, unpublished).

Burney, E. (1980) *A Chance to Change*, Howard League.

Carlen, P. (1976) *Magistrates' Justice*, London, Martin Robertson.

Carlen, P. (1983a) 'On Rights and Powers: Notes on Penal Politics', in D. Garland and P. Young (eds), *The Power to Punish*, London, Heinemann Educational.

Carlen, P. (1983b) *Women's Imprisonment*, London, Routledge & Kegan Paul.

Carlen, P. and Powell, M. (1979) 'Professionals in the Magistrates' Court', in H. Parker (ed.), *Social Work and the Courts*, London, Edward Arnold.

Casburn, M. (1979) *Girls will be Girls*, London, WRRC.

Central Council of Probation Committees (1981) 'Future Problems – The Pattern of Female Crime' (Ref. 7/7, unpublished).

Chambliss, W. J. (1971) 'A Sociological Analysis of the Law of Vagrancy', in W. G. Carson and P. Wiles (eds), *Crime and Delinquency in Britain*, London, Martin Robertson.

CHAR (1983) *Fraud and Operation Major: an Assessment*, London.

Coggan, G. and Walker, M. (1982) *Frightened for my Life*, Glasgow, Fontana.

Collins, S. and Behan, D. (1981) *Social Work with Young Offenders*, London, Butterworth.

Corden, J. (1983) 'Persistent Petty Offenders: Problems and Patterns of Multiple Disadvantage', *Howard Journal*, XXII.

Corrigan, P. and Leonard, P. (1978) *Social Work Practice Under Capital-*

*ism: A Marxist Approach*, London, Macmillan.

Cromar, P. (1983) 'Industry', in P. Lee (ed.), 'Banishing Dark Divisive Clouds', *Critical Social Policy*, issue 8.

Davies, B. (1982) 'Towards a Personalist Framework for Radical Social Work Education', in R. Bailey and P. Lee (eds), *Theory and Practice in Social Work*, Oxford, Blackwell.

Dobash, R. and Dobash, R. (1979) *Violence Against Wives*, London, Open Books.

Emerson, R. M. (1967) *Judging Delinquents*, Chicago, Aldine.

Farrington, D. and Morris, A. (1983) 'Sex, Sentencing and Reconviction', *British Journal of Criminology*, vol. 23, no. 3.

Fitzgerald, M. (1977) *Prisoners in Revolt*, Harmondsworth, Penguin.

Franey, R. (1983) *Poor Law*, London, CHAR, CPAG, Claimants' Defence Committee, NAPO, NCCL.

Freire, P. (1972) *Pedagogy of the Oppressed*, Harmondsworth, Penguin.

Freire, P. (1976) 'A Few Notions about the Word "Conscientisation"', in *Schooling and Capitalism*, London, Routledge & Kegan Paul, in association with the Open University.

Goldstein, H. (1973) *Social Work Practice: A Unitary Approach*, University of South Carolina Press.

Gordon, P. (1983) *White Law*, London, Pluto Press.

Greenwood, V. (1982) 'The Role and Future of Women's Imprisonment', Noel Buxton Lecture (unpublished).

Hall, S. (1983) 'The Great Moving Right Show', in S. Hall and M. Jacques (eds), *The Politics of Thatcherism*, London, Lawrence & Wishart.

Harding, J. (1982) *Victims and Offenders*, London, Bedford Square Press/NCVO.

Haxby, D. (1978) *Probation: A Changing Service*, London, Constable.

Hay, D. (1975) 'Property, Authority and the Criminal Law', in D. Hay, P. Linebaugh, J. Rule, E. P. Thompson and C. Winslow (eds), *Albion's Fatal Tree*, London, Allen Lane.

Heap, K. (1977) *Group Theory for Social Workers*, Oxford, Holywell Press.

Hedges, N. and Benyon, H. (1982) *Born to Work*, London, Pluto Press.

Heidenson, F. (1981) 'Women and the Penal System', in A. Morris and L. Gelsthorpe (eds), *Women and Crime*, Cambridge, Cropwood Conference Series, no. 13.

HMSO (1984) *The Government Reply to the First Report of the Education, Science and Arts Committee, 'Prison Education'*, Cmnd. 9126.

Hobsbawm, E. (1983) 'The Falklands Factor' in S. Hall and M. Jacques (eds), *The Politics of Thatcherism*, London, Lawrence & Wishart.

Home Office (1967) Circular 130/1967.

Home Office (1977) 'National Activity Recording Study', (unpublished).

Home Office (1979) *Life Sentence Prisoners*, Research Study no. 51, London, HMSO.

Home Office (1981) *Day Centres and Probation*, Research Paper 4, London, HMSO.

Home Office (1983a) *The British Crime Survey*, Research Study No. 76, London, HMSO.

Home Office (1983b) *Criminal Statistics, England and Wales*, Cmnd. 9048, London, HMSO.

Home Office (1983c) *Prison Statistics, England and Wales*, Cmnd. 9027, London, HMSO.

Home Office (1984) 'Statement of National Objectives and Priorities' (unpublished).

Howe, A., Johnson, B., Purser, B. and Read, G. (1982) 'Establishing Day Centres', *Probation Journal*, vol. 29, no. 2.

Ireland, M. and Dawes, J. (1975) 'Working with the Client in the Family', *Probation Journal*, vol. 22, no. 4.

Jarvis, P. (1983) *Adult and Continuing Education: Theory and Practice*, London, Croom Helm.

Jones, C. (1983) 'Thatcherism and the Attack on Expectations', *Bulletin on Social Policy*, no. 14.

Kemp, D. (1983) 'Prisoners and the Mental Health Act', *Prison Service Journal*, vol. 51 (July).

King, J. (1969) *The Probation and After-care Service*, London, Butterworth.

King, R. and Morgan, R. (1980) *The Future of the Prison System*, Aldershot, Gower.

Lacey, W. (1983) 'Thou Shalt Not Recommend Custody', *NAPO Newsletter* (August) no. 221.

Lee, P. (1983) 'Banishing Dark Divisive Clouds', *Critical Social Policy*, issue 8.

Lees, R. (1972) *Politics and Social Work*, London, Routledge & Kegan Paul.

Leicestershire Probation and After-care Service (1983) 'Information for the Sentencing Court' (unpublished).

Leivers, J. (1980) 'A Study of some Adolescent Groups in the Probation Service', *Probation Journal*, vol. 27 no. 1.

Lippitt, R. and White, R. K. (1958) 'An Experimental Study of Leadership and Group Life', in E. E. Maccoby *et al.*, *Readings in Social Psychology*, New York, Holt.

McCarthy, J. (1981) 'The Modern Prison', in J. Jones (ed.), *Society Against Crime*, Harmondsworth, Penguin.

McCaughan, N. (ed.) (1978) *Groupwork: Learning and Practice*, London, Allen & Unwin.

McGrath, S. (1983) 'The CHAR Blueprint: Its relevance for the Probation Service', *Probation Journal*, vol. 30, no. 3.

McLeod, E. (1981) 'Man-made Laws for Men? The Street Prostitutes' Campaign Against Control', in B. Hutter and G. Williams (eds), *Controlling Women*, London, Croom Helm.

McLeod, E. (1982) *Working Women: Prostitution Now*, London, Croom Helm.

McLeod, E. and Dominelli, L. (1982) 'The Personal and the Apolitical', in R. Bailey and P. Lee (eds), *Theory and Practice in Social Work*, Oxford, Blackwell.

McShane, D. (1979) *Using the Media*, London, Pluto Press.

Manpower Services Commission (1983) *Annual Report.*

Mathieson, T. (1974) *The Politics of Abolition*, London, Martin Robertson.

Mathieson, T. (1980) *Law, Society and Political Action*, London, Academic Press.

Mawby, R. I. (1977) 'Sexual Discrimination and the Law', *Probation Journal*, vol. 24, no. 2.

Mitra, C. (1983) Letter to *Community Care* (23 September 1983).

Morison Report (1962) *Report of the Departmental Committee on the Probation Service*, Cmnd. 1650, London, HMSO.

Morris, A. and Gelsthorpe, L. (1981) 'False Clues and Female Crime', in A. Morris and L. Gelsthorpe (eds), *Women and Crime*, Cambridge, Cropwood Conference Series, no. 13.

Morris, T. (1978) 'The Parlous State of Prisons' in J. Freeman (ed.), *Prisons: Past and Future*, London, Heinemann.

NACRO (1978a) *Memorandum to the House of Commons Expenditure Committee into the Penal System.*

NACRO (1978b) *Notes on Running a Wives' Group.*

NACRO (1981) *Women in the Penal System.*

NACRO (1983a) *The Resettlement of Ex-offenders: Towards a New Approach.*

NACRO (1983b) *Forgotten Victims: How Prison Affects the Family.*

NACRO (1983c) *Briefing: Women in Prison.*

NAPO (1980) *Constitution.*

NAPO (1983a) 'The Future Provision for the Through-care Needs of Prisoners' (unpublished).

NAPO (1983b) *Newsletter* (March) no. 216.

Nelson, S. (1982) *Incest: Fact and Myth*, Edinburgh, Stramullion.

Parkinson, G. (1983) 'Tailgunner Parkinson', *New Society*, (1 September 1983).

Parsloe, P. (1972) 'Why don't Probation Officers run client groups?', *Probation*, vol. 18, no. 1.

Pearce, I. and Wareham, A. (1977) 'The Questionable Relevance of Research into Social Enquiry Reports', *Howard Journal*, vol. 16, no. 2.

Perry, T. and Burnham, D. (1977) 'The Mansfield Homelessness Project', *Social Work Today*, vol. 9, no. 14.

Pincus A. and Minahan, A. (1973) *Social Work Practice: Model and Method*, Illinois, Peacock Press.

Pond, C. (1983) 'Taxation' in P. Lee (ed.) 'Banishing Dark Divisive Clouds', *Critical Social Policy*, issue 8.

Pratt, M. (1975) 'Stress and Opportunity in the Role of the Prison Welfare Officer', *British Journal of Social Work*, vol. 5, no. 4.

Priestley, P. *et al.* (1978) *Social Skills and Personal Problem Solving*, London, Tavistock.

Purser, B., Howe, A., Hopkins, T., Johnson, B. (1982) *Probation Day Care: A Guide to Basics*, Midland Region Staff Development.

Radical Alternatives to Prison (1972) *Alternatives to Holloway*, London, RAP.

Rothman, B. and Papell, C. P. (1977) 'Social Groupwork Models: Possession and Heritage', in H. Specht and A. Vickery (eds), *Integrating Social Work Methods*, London, Allen & Unwin.

Salmon, H. (1983) *Unemployment: Government Schemes and Alternatives*, Association of Community Workers.

Seddon, V. (1981) 'Violence Against Women: male power in action', *Marxism Today* (August).

Smart, C. (1976) *Women, Crime and Criminology*, London, Routledge & Kegan Paul.

Smart, C. (1981) 'Law and the Control of Women's Sexuality', in B. Hutter and G. Williams (eds), *Controlling Women*, London, Croom Helm.

Smart, C. and Smart, B. (1978) 'Accounting for Rape', in C. Smart and B. Smart (eds), *Women, Sexuality and Social Control*, London, Routledge & Kegan Paul.

Smith, D. (1979) 'Probation Officers in Prison', in D. Brandon and B. Jordan (eds), *Creative Social Work*, Oxford, Blackwell.

Spender, D. (1980) *Man Made Language*, London, Routledge & Kegan Paul.

Stanley, L. and Wise, S. (1983) *Breaking Out: feminist consciousness and feminist research*, London, Routledge & Kegan Paul.

Stone, N. (1981) 'New Directions for Probation', *Justice of the Peace* (14 November 1981).

Stone, N. (1982) 'Swings and Roundabouts: The Current State of Prison Welfare', *Prison Service Journal* (April).

Stone, N. (1984) 'The Home Secretary: An Interview', *Probation Journal*, vol. 31, no. 1.

Taylor, I. (1981) *Law and Order: Arguments for Socialism*, London, Macmillan.

Taylor, L. (1978) 'Ethics and Expediency in Penal Practice' in J. Freeman (ed.), *Prisons: Past and Future*, London, Heinemann.

Thomas, H. A. (1982) 'The Road to Custody is Paved with Good Intentions', *Probation Journal*, vol. 29, no. 3.

Thorpe, D. H., Smith, D., Green, C. J., Paley, J. H. (1980) *Out of Care*, London, Allen & Unwin.

Tolson, A. (1977) *The Limits of Masculinity*, London, Tavistock.

Trevelyan, D. (1982) 'New and Current Problems in Execution of Sentences of Imprisonment', Lecture to the International Penal and Penitentiary Foundation, Siracusa (February 1982, unpublished).

Unemployment Unit (1982) *Briefing Paper No. 4*, (October ).

Walker, H. and Beaumont, B. (1981) *Probation Work: Critical Theory and Socialist Practice*, Oxford, Blackwell.

Walker, N. (1984) 'On the Clapper: Comments on the Past Year', *Probation Journal*, vol. 31, no. 1.

Ward, T. (1982) 'Towards Abolition', *The Abolitionist*, no. 12.

Wener, G. (1983) *A Legitimate Grievance: A Report on the Role of the Ombudsman in the Prison System*, London, Prison Reform Trust.

West Midlands Probation Service (1981) *Probation and After-Care in a Multi-Racial Society*, London, Commission for Racial Equality.

Whitehouse, P. (1983) 'Race, Bias and Social Enquiry Reports', *Probation Journal*, vol. 30, no. 2.

Whitlock, S. (1983) 'By Women and for Women', *Social Work Today*, vol. 14, no. 30.

Wilkinson, B., Cherry, S. and Williams, S. (1981) 'Women and Criminality', *Probe* (February).

Wilson, E. (1977) *Women and the Welfare State*, London, Tavistock.

Wilson, E. (1980) 'Feminism and Social Work', in M. Brake and R. Bailey (eds) *Radical Social Work and Practice*, London, Edward Arnold.

Wilson, E. (1983) *What is to be Done about Violence Against Women?*, Harmondsworth, Penguin.

Winfield, M. and Riddick, M. (1983) *Links or Chains? A Guide to Community Involvement with Prisons*, London, Prison Reform Trust.

Woodroofe, K. (1962) *From Charity to Social Work*, London, Routledge & Kegan Paul.

Worrall, A. (1981) 'Out of Place: Female Offenders in Court', *Probation Journal*, vol. 28, no. 3.

Younger Report (1974) *Young Adult Offenders. A Report of the Advisory Council on the Penal System*, London, HMSO.

# Notes on Contributors

*Bill Beaumont* has worked as a probation officer in London since 1970. He is an active NAPO member and was Chair of NAPO 1981–4. He is the co-author of *Probation Work: Critical Theory and Socialist Practice* (1981).

*Paul James* has worked as a probation officer in Coventry and Nuneaton since 1971 and is an active member of NAPO and the NAPO Members' Action Group. He has specialised in work with voluntary community projects, most recently in a day centre.

*Kevin Kirwin* has worked as a probation officer in London since 1978, having previously been a probation ancillary. He is an active member of NAPO and the NAPO Members' Action Group.

*Margaret Powell* was a probation officer in London 1971–9, then a lecturer in social work at Middlesex Polytechnic 1979–82 before returning to work as a probation officer in Avon. She was a contributor to *Social Work and the Courts* (1979) and is an active NAPO member.

*Paul Senior* worked as a probation officer in Doncaster 1976–82 where he built up extensive experience in group work. He now holds a joint appointment as a lecturer in social work at Sheffield City Polytechnic and senior probation officer in South Yorkshire. He is an active NAPO member.

*Nigel Stone* worked as a probation officer in Nottinghamshire 1974–9 before taking up his present joint appointment as lecturer in social work at the University of East Anglia and probation officer in Norfolk. Between 1979–82 he was based part time in Norwich prison. He is an active NAPO member and since 1982 has been editor of *Probation Journal.*

*Hilary Walker* worked as a probation officer in Middlesex and Leicester for six years. She is the co-author of *Probation Work: Critical Theory and Socialist Practice* (1981). Since 1981 she has worked mainly with women and children in a Camden Social Services young family care centre.

# Index

## 150 *Index*